LINCOLN BIBLE INSTITUTE

P9-CRN-007

LIVING CAN BE EXCITING

By Aaron N. Meckel

NEW DAY FOR EVANGELISM

LIVING CAN BE EXCITING

E·P·DUTTON&CO.INC
EST. 1852
OVER 100 YEARS OF CREATIVE PUBLISHING

Living

CAN BE EXCITING

By Aaron N. Meckel

✝

Foreword by
HALFORD E. LUCCOCK

E. P. DUTTON & COMPANY, INC.

NEW YORK, 1956

Copyright, ©, *1956*, by E. P. Dutton & Co., Inc.
All rights reserved. Printed in the U. S. A.

FIRST EDITION

¶ *No part of this book may be reproduced
in any form without permission in writing
from the publisher, except by a reviewer
who wishes to quote brief passages in con-
nection with a review written for inclusion in
magazine or newspaper or radio broadcast.*

LIBRARY OF CONGRESS CATALOG CARD NUMBER: 56-8282

252.058
M48

gift

Sept 57

11

12910

For

LILLIAN

FOREWORD

by

HALFORD E. LUCCOCK

IF "LIVING CAN BE EXCITING," so can preaching! And
here, in lively pages, is animated proof.

These sermons of Dr. Meckel's have simplicity and
force; they retain to a remarkable degree qualities of
the spoken word which for years have held overflow
audiences in his church at St. Petersburg, Florida. He
has held his audience as firmly as The Ancient Mariner,
but not by "his glittering eye." I have never noticed
whether Aaron Meckel's eye glitters or not, but I *have*
noticed that he holds people by vigorous speech.

I have enjoyed these sermons for many reasons but
first because of their directness. They waste no time
in shadow boxing. They go to the mark of their subject like a bullet and do not spray the universe with
words. And they end up with a sharp point like a
bayonet, not like a broom.

Another source of enjoyment and profit is clear,
comprehensible style. Dr. Meckel does not speak in the
theological jargon so common in many pulpits today,
a sort of ecclesiastical equivalent of "gobbledegook."

7

Foreword

Much preaching in our day is cursed by murkiness and muddiness, ideas cast in a theological code apparently designed to keep the high meaning a secret. Just as serious literary criticism has lost touch with the general public, so much preaching is being done not for the public but for a coterie. Yet man cannot live by bread alone or by a diet of Kierkegaard and existentialism. Such jargon is too much like this scientific definition: "A kiss is the anatomical juxtaposition of two orbicular muscles in a state of contraction." No doubt. But a kiss can be described more persuasively and appealingly.

Dr. Meckel treats subjects of first importance. He is alive to his time both in his choice of subjects and in their treatment.

Best of all, there is emphatic Christian message in these sermons. A cartoon a few months ago unintentionally had much to do with preaching. It showed a historical scene, the runner from the Battle of Marathon bringing news of the victory to Athens. A group of Athenian city fathers was waiting in strained anxiety. The runner arrived, carrying a torch, and gasped out, "I've forgotten the message."

Dr. Meckel does not forget the message. The reader of this book will not forget it either.

CONTENTS

Page

FOREWORD, HALFORD E. LUCCOCK   7

Chapter

1. THERE IS HEALING IN LAUGHTER   13

2. IS PEACE OF MIND ENOUGH?   25

3. TO DRINK OR NOT TO DRINK   37

4. HOW SHALL WE THINK OF OUR DEPARTED ONES? 51

5. I STILL BELIEVE IN PEOPLE!   65

6. GO INTO THE SILENCE AND LISTEN!   78

7. HOW DOES ONE LEARN TO HAVE FAITH?   91

8. MAKE YOUR HANDICAP SERVE!   105

9. SOMETIMES UP AND SOMETIMES DOWN   116

10. DYING THE LITTLE DEATHS   126

11. STAND UP AND BE COUNTED!   138

12. "THE BEST IS YET TO BE"—WHY GROW OLD? 152

13. THE WAY OUT OF OUR WORRIES   166

14. THE REAL MEANING OF HAPPINESS   178

15. PRAYER, THE SOLUTION TO ALL OUR PROBLEMS 191

16. MAKING YOUR MARRIAGE A HAPPY ONE   204

17. KEEP GRATITUDE ALIVE IN YOUR HEART   217

18. WHAT ARE YOU EXPECTING?   228

19. WHY FEAR DEATH?   239

LIVING CAN BE EXCITING

Chapter 1

THERE IS HEALING IN LAUGHTER

"Blessed is the people that know the joyful sound."

(Psalm 89: 15*)*

IN A FORUM discussion entitled *THIS I BELIEVE,* Sir Hugh Casson, noted British architect, gives his reasons for parting with much conventional religion. "Perhaps, I don't know, it is the atmosphere of death in which religion is so steeped that has discouraged me—the graveyards, the parsonical voice, the thin damp smell of stone." And he adds that to this very day a "holy" face is to his mind morose, rather than saintly.[1]

Granted that Sir Hugh's complaint is somewhat exaggerated: nevertheless, there is much truth in what he says. You have only to mention the subject of religion in some circles and the response is a lowered brow and a look of pity! You may even be regarded as an old fogey or a kill-joy. If it be true, as L. P. Jacks has said, that today there is a "lost radiance of religion,"

[1] Edward Murrow, *This I Believe* (New York: Simon & Schuster), p. 27.

13

then it is likewise true that modern living has lost its real raison d'être. Many people in our day simply would not recognize the genuine "article" should they chance upon it. They do not seem to understand that the Christian faith, as Dr. Fosdick has put it, is "not weight, but *wings*;" that, without it, life lacks zest, joy, and meaning.

True, one occasionally comes upon some rather dreary exhibitions of the real thing. Consider the service I attended in a large Southern church. After the sermon a little boy was called forward to be received into the church as a member. What can be more exciting than the experience of becoming a member of Christ's flock when the real significance of that step dawns on one? And yet, on that day, my heart sank as the minister read from a long and cumbersome ritual. Did this little eight-year-old renounce the world, the flesh, and the devil? That may be a fitting question for older people, but what, after all, does a mere child know about such things? Nothing happened that day to gladden the heart of a little boy who was joining the thrilling ranks of Jesus' followers. I imagined the Master putting a kindly arm about that boy and saying, "Welcome into My church! You and I will walk along through life together as close friends. Trust in Me, and rejoice."

Our religion needs to have its "face lifted." We need to get back to the religion of Jesus Christ which was pre-eminently a religion of joy. It was not staid, stereo-typed and stuffy but filled with faith and gladness. Today, far too much of our preaching is moralistic in tone, our worship monotonous, and our music funereal. Gerald Kennedy suggests that Christian ministers would do well to reread the Christmas story every Sunday before entering the pulpit. That story is one of joy.

Wherever you come across a person who has really caught the infection of the Good News, you find genuine, unalloyed joy. Some of you have read John Gunther's account of his visit to Albert Schweitzer in Lambaréné, Africa. He could not forget the sound of Schweitzer's laughter. It had none of the death rattle of the cynic. When the great missionary laughed, you could hear the gurgle of a pure mountain stream and the spontaneous glee of an unspoiled aborigine.

After hearing Beethoven's *Fifth Symphony*, Claudel, the French poet, said that he knew that there was eternal joy at the heart of the universe.

There is, then, such a thing as a "deep down laughter" of the heart. The Psalmist of Israel mentions it when he says, "Blessed is the people who have heard the joyful sound!"

If anyone has a right to be happy it is the Christian. A lusterless Christian is a contradiction in terms. The follower of the great Nazarene knows that there is healing in laughter. Let us see why that is true.

I

Genuine "deep down" laughter brings healing for troubled minds and sick bodies. "The merry heart," said the writer of the Proverbs, "doeth good like a medicine." (Prov. 17:22). Laughter is a spiritual herb we all need to take occasionally.

The world of literature has taken that need seriously to heart. Look into the format of many a modern magazine or paper and you will find a place for humor. "Laughter is the best medicine" is a common adage. Modern life is hurried and hectic in pace. It is hard, metallic, and competitive. As a result, many people have forgotten *how* to laugh. They need release from nagging worries, besetting anxieties, and tensions which have tied them into emotional knots. The angels of our better nature are often in eclipse. We need the therapy of laughter.

Listen, for instance, to the poignant plea of Louise Fletcher Tarkington, in her poem, *The Land of Beginning Again:*

> For there isn't a sting that will not take wing
> When we've faced it and laughed it away,
> And I think that the laughter is most what we're after
> In the Land of Beginning Again.

She would agree with these words of Olive Schreiner

that "the echoes of despair slink away, for the laughter
of a brave, strong heart is death to them."

Not only the world of literature, the magazine
writers and the poets, but the world of entertainment
caters to the hunger for a "deep down" kind of laughter. Just turn on your radio or television set! Mirth has
become a commodity, retailed at so many laughs a
minute. The commercial funsters and jokesters are
riding the crest. We even have "laugh meters" register-
ing the ability of an entertainer to make his audience
happy. Many a man who will not set foot in church
will sit by the hour and listen to the pranks of Bob
Hope, Red Skelton, Gracie Allen, George Gobel, and
others.

In time of war we send someone like Bob Hope to
entertain our American men and boys abroad. They
are tired, battle-scarred, and homesick. They need to
"laugh their troubles" away—at least for a few hours.
Businessmen enjoy going to their club luncheons and
singing about "packing up their troubles in their old
kit bags" and smiling again!

We have underrated the place of laughter in our
religion. Wiser in their generation are the children of
this world, than are some children of God! Martin
Luther said that he created hymns because he refused
to allow the devil to have all the good tunes! A pastor-
friend of mine includes the words, "Remember, religion
has a smile," in his Saturday church notices. Thomas de

Witt Talmage, famous preacher of a generation ago, gave as his opinion that "one good hearty laugh is a bombshell exploding in the right place, while spleen and discontent are a gun that kicks over the man who shoots it off."

A friend of mine remembers something that was said by the president of his Rotary Club at the time America entered the Second World War. "I want to hear a lot of laughter around here," said this Rotary head, "for we shall be needing it more than ever." He added, "A nation that can keep its sense of humor has the best chance to win."

I believe that that is far more than just good Rotarianism; it is good religion. Jesus came that His joy might be in us and that our joy might be full. When that joy gets inside a man's heart it relieves crippling tension, releases latent capacities, and allows God-given life forces to flow unhindered through him. There is healing in laughter.

II

Furthermore, genuine laughter is also an indication of emotional maturity: a sign that one has come into his spiritual majority. A man with a sense of humor usually sees life "steadily and sees it whole." As Dr. Rollo May has said, such a man has a way of standing

off and looking at his problem with perspective.[2]
Anxiety and fear have not gotten him down so long as
he can laugh. He possesses the qualities of an essential
human being.

Someone saw an elderly Negro sitting on a fence
and laughing at the top of his voice. "If you white folks
could just sit here and see yourselves walking by, you
would laugh yourselves to death!" he said.

If only Hitler had gotten a good look at himself, he
might have burst into laughter and so might have spared
the world the scourge of Nazism. But Herrenvolk cannot laugh or engage in humor. *That* would be a sign
of weakness! Nazism and Communism and their ilk are
grim and rigid.

Was not Thackeray describing such men when he
said: "Stupid people who do not know how to laugh
are always pompous and self-conceited: that is, un-
gentle, uncharitable, unchristian."

The many strained and drawn faces one sees in these
days are a sure sign that many of us are taking ourselves
too seriously. We do not let the rich joy of life pour
itself out in us. We want to fit into other's expectations
of us rather than be our own free spontaneous selves.
But when God puts laughter into the depths of a man's
soul, he becomes gloriously free from pretense and
make-believe. He is no longer afflicted with a perfec-
tionist complex. He can afford to be his own best self.

---

[2] Rollo May, *Man's Search for Himself*, p. 61.

And if he is a Christian, he knows himself to be a sinner saved by grace. Once a man stands *there*, he is close to the heart and reality of things. He experiences the inner gaiety and winsomeness of the saints.

As Christians, we do not wear a smile on our faces, nor are we inwardly gay in order to "win friends and influence people." God has spilled His joy into our hearts and we cannot but be joyful! We have learned to count our blessings and find them many. We have looked into the heart of life and found it good. The opposite of joy is not sorrow but unbelief.

Persons brimming over with good will prove to be a real blessing in tense and explosive situations. During a meeting of the World Council of Churches in Evanston, Illinois, speaker after speaker rose with grave complicated proposals. It was a hot sticky afternoon and tempers were getting testy. Nerves were on edge; things seemed to have arrived at stalemate. In the presiding chair sat pink-cheeked Geoffry Francis Fisher, Primate of England and Archbishop of Canterbury. Presently, he spoke: "I think I shall put to vote only the last of several proposals made, because it's the only one I can remember." He paused, grinning. "By the way," he said, "what was it?"

A round of laughter rolled out over the large hall. Tension was transformed into easy informality. This man, with the scholar's mind and a boy's sunny heart, saved the day.

A friend of mine was growing irritable as he drove along in heavy week-end traffic. He was about to lose his temper when he observed a sign scrawled on the back of an old jalopy, the proud possession of a college student. It read, "Go ahead and honk; it's your ulcer!" That sign saved the day.

III

But we have yet to mention the main raison d'être for the Christian's inner laughter. He has *something to be really glad about*. It is something that keeps his heart singing in the midst of all "the still sad music of humanity" he hears around him. God's mighty saving act in Jesus Christ has penetrated his being. He has discovered in Christ the "expulsive power of a new affection." This joy of the Christian is the primitive, authentic kind which never fades. You can find the facsimile of it in a great hymn like Horatio Bonar's, *I Heard the Voice of Jesus Say*. The weary man responds to the invitation of Jesus and comes into a true sense of life's meaning as he sings:

> I came to Jesus as I was,
> Weary and worn and sad;
> I found in Him a resting place,
> And He has made me glad.

Emerson Bradshaw speaks of Kagawa as "the saint

who laughs." The great Japanese Christian has tasted the dregs of life. He knows the meaning of poor physical health and of suffering as few know it. Yet he is possessed of an infectious gaiety that readily communicates itself to everyone around him. During one of his American tours a university student arose, and with an air of bravado, asked, "Why bother with all this talk about religion—religion has busted up." Kagawa answered simply: "Mine hasn't."

When Rufus Moseley became a Christian, Christ somehow filled him with an irrepressible flow of laughter. He quite literally laughed his way through life. He had an inner fountain that bubbled. Some rather dour persons failed to see the point of this new-found joy and put him down as an eccentric. But Christ's fool went right on laughing. A couple who had taken him into their home during a conference were a bit disturbed over his constant hilarity of spirit. However, after he had been their guest for a week, the husband said to his wife, "There may be someone 'crazy' around here, but it isn't Brother Rufus!"

IV

Notice also that the man who has learned to laugh rests the burden of the world's woes and sorrows back on the heart of the Eternal. In the midst of war, revolu-

tion, fear, and unrest, he travels light. He believes there
is "a great, divine event towards which the whole
creation moves," and that nothing can stop it. He
knows that the ultimate victory over evil and death
in this world has been decisively won in the death and
resurrection of Jesus Christ. As a follower of the Master,
he has personally appropriated that victory. He believes
it, lives it, shares it.

It was my good fortune to attend a chaplain's con-
vocation during the days of the Second World War.
These men had looked upon and shared untold suffering and destruction and death. Had they looked at life
through sour eyes, it would not have been surprising.
On the contrary, you should have heard them laugh!
They were still glad to be alive and serve their fellowmen. The glad zest of life was in them. The world might
be in a mess; but a voice sounded through the tumult
and confusion of the hour, saying, "Be of good cheer,
I have overcome the world." And they believed that
voice.

Jesus went out from the Upper Room, on the night
in which He was betrayed, to face the cup with a song
on His lips.

The first Christian martyrs entered the Roman arena
with hymns of praise to Christ.

The saints of the church, both great and small, went
about humble tasks with merry heart. St. Francis of
Assisi sang his joy into the soul of an age that had

surrendered its birthright of happiness. Think of Brother Lawrence, praising the Lord as he passed the dishes in the kitchen of the monastery where he served. Recall Paul, writing his glorious letters from a Roman prison and saying, "Rejoice, and again I say, rejoice!" Which of us can recall these saints and not agree that "Joy is the grace we say to God!"

Suppose we sum up what we have tried to say about the healing power of laughter: It releases tensions within us and makes way for the healing power of God to flow through us again. It is an evident sign of spiritual and emotional maturity in the laugher. Christ Himself is the authentic source and fountain of that laughter. The believer knows that God is still on the throne, and that, in the end, God's Kingdom shall surely come.

Life still is good for the one who can go his way, scattering sunshine and good will, like Pippa in Robert Browning's famous poem:

> The year's at the spring,
> The day's at the morn;
> Morning's at seven:
> The hill-side's dew-pearled;
> The lark's on the wing;
> The snail's on the thorn;
> God's in His heaven:
> All's right with the world!

Chapter 2

IS PEACE OF MIND ENOUGH?

"Therefore being justified by faith, we have peace
with God through our Lord Jesus Christ."

(*Rom.* 5:1)

IN HIS BOOK *Peace of Mind*, Joshua Loth Liebman tells
how, in the brashness of his youth, he once undertook
to draw up a list of the goods which constitute life's
summum bonum. Talent, power, success, riches, fame,
health, and beauty—these were but part of the list. He
then went to an aged spiritual mentor and showed him
what he had written. The old man's eyes shone with
evident interest as he read. Soon, however, he took a
pencil and drew a line through all these vaunted ele-
ments of success. In their place, he inscribed three
words and held them up for the younger man's scru-
tiny. The words were *Peace of Mind*. Without this
treasure, he said, all the others on the list would soon
canker and turn to worthless dust on a man's hands.

And the minted wisdom of the ancients would agree in saying, let the treasures of the world be heaped at the feet of fools, but let the truly wise man pray, "Grant me the gift of the untroubled mind."[1]

In our more pensive moments, we all yearn for this rarest of all God's gifts. We long to walk through the day without harassing doubts and fears; to saunter out into nature and to hold communion with "her visible forms"; to walk among our friends and associates in the spirit of true camaraderie; and to be able to trust ourselves under all circumstances. In a word, we long to possess that incomparable gift, than which there is no greater—the gift of the untroubled mind!

Were any further evidence of this yearning needed, we could point to the contemporary proliferation of cults, the growing popularity of novenas and retreats, and the trek of distressed persons to the offices of psychological and religious consultants. All these are indications of man's yearning for inward serenity.

Of late, however, a question has intruded itself. Is this so-called "peace of mind" enough? In line with this question is still another asked by Dr. Paul Hutchinson in *Life Magazine*, April 11, 1955: Have we a "new" religion on our hands? Dr. Hutchinson appears to think so and refers to it as a cult of reassurance. This cult, furthermore, has its high priests, its millions of devotees,

1 Joshua Loth Liebman, *Peace of Mind* (New York: Simon & Schuster), p. 3.

its widely distributed literature, and its ritual. Hutchinson is willing to admit that some definite good has been accomplished by this "new" religion, that it is far from being an unmitigated evil. Nevertheless, along with many others, he feels that something essential to our great Hebrew-Christian heritage is being left out. If so, what is it?

With that question in mind, I turned to my New Testament and reread the inner heart-message of the gospel. In this chapter I want to tell you what I found. The promise of peace is indeed there, for did not Jesus explicitly say, "My peace I give unto you?" (John 14:27). That peace, however, was not the makeshift peace of the secular world but His very own gift to the believer. Its sole source is in God.

One comes away from a careful study of the New Testament with renewed conviction that the peace delineated in its pages is part of a larger gift of life and that there are some definite demands on those who would share this treasure. "Since then," writes St. Paul, "it is by faith that we are justified, let us grasp the fact that we *have* peace with God through our Lord Jesus Christ." (Rom. 5:1, J. B. Phillips trans.). When he spoke these words, the great Apostle cut through all outer sham to the inward meaning of peace. That peace—that gift of the untroubled heart—may be the precious possession of everyone.

I

Primarily, I have found that this gift of inner serenity stems from a new and vital relationship with God.
It involves an act of commitment on our part as a result
of which God, in his great love, accepts us as his very
own.

There can be no short cut to this paradise! There is a
price to pay. "Take what you want," says an old
Spanish proverb, "take it and pay for it." There is basic
and fundamental "spade work" to be accomplished in
a man's life before he can taste the joy of inward
release, and apart from which religion loses the dimension of profundity and dwindles into a cult of self-
improvement.

Cultism seeks the easy way out of our difficulties. It
offers to teach the art of living in "twelve brief lessons."
Cultism skims the surface of need, makes superficial
diagnoses, mistakes symptoms for causes. The unpleas-
ant fact of sin in a life is shunted aside. Cultism asks,
"What do I get out of it?" Profound religion, on the
other hand, has a much deeper basis of motivation, for
it asks, "What must I bring?" "What must I do to be
saved?"

Years ago I made the acquaintance of a man who was
always shopping for a new religion. We might call him
a fringe religionist. He was one of the many in our

day who skip like the fabled ram from one cult to another, "ever learning and never able to come to the knowledge of the truth." (II Tim. 3:7). The cult which was the vogue at the time, which advertised its wares the most blatantly and made the least demands of its devotee—that was it. I can still remember this man puffing away at his cigarette and ridiculing Jesus and His stern but kindly demand for faith and repentance.

Suppose that on the memorable night of their interview, Jesus had said to Nicodemus, "Now, my good man, there is nothing radically wrong with you, you are just scrupulous!" Not so did our Lord deal with the ruler of the Jews. Instead He pierced to the inner heart-hunger and need of this man before Him, insisting that he must be born again through the power of the Spirit. In like manner, He dealt with the rich young ruler, the young man of exemplary moral character, who, aware of his inner discontent, came asking what he still lacked. Jesus immediately put His finger on the place of greatest need: "You lack one thing; go, sell what you have, and give to the poor, and you will have treasure in heaven; and come, follow me." (Mark 10:21, R.S.V.). So human it is to want one thing and to need another! The Great Physician presses home the claims of God on the souls of those who come to Him asking for the gift of life. In the words of the old hymn it is the way of the cross that leads home.

Let me make myself plain. Certainly there is nothing

morbid about the salvation Jesus Christ offers the believer. The exact opposite is the truth. The most joyous experience that a man can undergo is that of becoming a Christian! No self-condemnation or self-reproach are called for. The moment any of us turn with simple, heartfelt yearning to God, light fills our hearts and darkness falls behind us. Viewed in this light, peace of mind is the result of a new and vital relationship with God, through faith. Life is set in right relationships with God. That is what being justified means.

Dr. A. J. Cronin, in his autobiography *Adventures in Two Worlds*, describes his adventure into the new life of faith in words which are reminiscent of Bunyan's *Pilgrim's Progress*. The Hound of Heaven had finally tracked him down. His outer defences and the tawdry rationalizations behind which he had hid for years, crumbled. His period of rebellion against heaven at last was ended. He felt the "inexorable appeal of the Cross." The famous physician-author is glad to share with us what he found:

There was fresh joy in my work. The sadness, tension and gnawing ennui which had assailed me all were gone. I had cried aloud and the sky had heard my cry. . . . I had made the immense discovery of why I was alive.[2]

[2] A. J. Cronin, *Adventures in Two Worlds*, (New York: McGraw-Hill), p. 278.

Is Peace Of Mind Enough?

When any of us make the discovery of life's true meaning, then *living becomes exciting*. Life's tangled skein is unraveled. We respond with all our being to God's great saving act in Jesus Christ. A new and dominant emotion of love, joy and gratitude takes possession of us. The soul inwardly capers and dances for sheer delight. Jesus' words ring out with new meaning: "Rejoice! For this my son was dead and is alive again: he was lost and is found!" We have come home by way of the cross!

II

Moreover, this deeper surgery of the Spirit we have been discussing is no mere elective but a deep inward necessity. It is a psychological imperative for the soul's health. In his famous *Confessions*, Augustine writes, "Thou madest us for Thyself, and we shall never find rest save as we rest in Thee." How well the young libertine knew whereof he spoke! After finding every other way to be a dead end, he eventually found peace with God through saving faith in Jesus Christ. Like the prodigal son, of whom Jesus spoke, he leaves home saying, "Father, give me," and returns again to the parental threshold a pathetic penitent, saying, "Father, make me as one of thy hired servants."

Rabbi Liebman's intentions in his famous book are easily misinterpreted. A superficial reading would seem to indicate that the author is the dispenser of a painless nostrum which he calls "peace of mind," and also that this gift can be won *apart from* the timeless disciplines of religion. Those who knew Dr. Liebman are aware that he never meant to give that impression. Wise student and counselor of troubled souls that he was, he knew that in religion, as elsewhere, short cuts are deceptive and that honest self-confrontation is necessary.

Read the second chapter entitled "Conscience Doth Make Cowards," and you become aware that, for the author, being religious is far more than a mild flirtation with deity. Let a man refuse to come to God by means of earnest self-examination and repentance, and the sense of guilt, which has been inwardly repressed, begins to be a psychic troublemaker. Failing to accept God's gift of forgiveness, he begins to "take it out" on himself through self-condemnation, and on others, through the subtle mechanism of projection. Although not a Christian, the great rabbi, nevertheless, realized the profound significance of repentance as revealed for instance in these words:

> . . . all the streets of the world are teeming with men and women who mutilate themselves spiritually and mentally in the invisible ways of self-criticism and self-degradation.[3]

[3] Liebman, *op. cit.*, p. 41.

32

Is Peace Of Mind Enough?

Alcoholism, drug addiction and sexual promiscuity are so many false attempts to find a way out of this psychic tangle. In Dr. Fosdick's phrase, we cease to be "fit to live with."

How many persons of this type there are, unwilling to face themselves on the deeper levels of their being and forever running away from life! They fetch up periodically in the minister's consultation room. Here, for instance, is the man who is unwilling to recognize God's claim on his life. He is the victim of a crippling sense of inferiority which he unconsciously "takes out" on himself and on his unfortunate companions. He is dying a slow death of spiritual attrition.

A classic instance of this type of individual is Willie Loman in Arthur Miller's, *Death of a Salesman*. Instead of achieving a coherent and stable selfhood through the disciplines of redemptive religion, he allows the pressures of society to hammer him into the rut of conformity. He engages in the game of make-believe. Willie's children get into trouble—lie and steal—but what of it? Do not some politicians in Washington, D. C., get ahead in much the same way? When Willie's employers finally turn him out to pasture, he cannot seem to understand their action.

After he finally takes his own life, a member of his family makes a revealing diagnosis of the deception at the heart of Willie's life: his friends were not to be too hard on him because——"he never knew who he was."

The great disciplines of prophetic, redemptive religion may appear stern to the uninitiated. But once they have been willingly accepted, their more kindly aspect becomes clear. Repentance is seen for what it is, not a backward but a forward-looking word. Above all, a man comes to know himself by means of it, and that self-knowledge confers on him the precious boon of the untroubled heart and the peace-filled mind.

III

One more thing about the peace of mind of which the New Testament speaks. Far from being the possession of an elect few, it is God's gracious gift to the unselfish of heart, to the burden-bearers of humanity! We keep it by giving it away. We find ourselves in the act of losing ourselves for Christ and the kingdom's sake. Thus, John Wesley kept insisting to his converts that the Bible knows nothing of solitary religion.

After his great experience of God's love and grace, Charles Haddon Spurgeon immediately sought to identify himself with God's people. Nothing could keep him from their midst: "I felt that I could not be happy without fellowship with the people of God." The grateful young Christian wanted not only to share in the gift of God's peace, but to be called by the name of the people of God, share their burdens, their very opprobrium, if necessary. Your Wesleys and Spurgeons knew from personal experience that having peace of mind is more than singing hymns within a sheltered circle. It might mean bearing heavy burdens and suffering severe persecution.

When Christian fellowship is genuine, our churches become oases of spiritual refreshment in the midst of the desert stretches of the world. Men enter into life as they join in the service and praise of God. And the enduring symbol of our faith is not only the Cross, central as that ever must be, but also the offering plate, as the sign that we devote ourselves to the redemption of mankind everywhere. *We are saved in order to serve.*

I like to revisit a little church which sits at the summit of a hill in one of our Midwestern cities. The church is named after a man who gave his entire life to the service of God and his fellows. Had you inquired of Francis Clarke the nature of his calling, he might well have replied in the words of William Carey: "My business is to be a Christian. I cobble shoes for a living."

He knew intimately the meaning of sorrow and bereavement. Yet, as you sat and talked with him, his eyes twinkled out of deep pools of serenity.

After his death, his daughter discovered the secret of her father's life among the personal keepsakes he had tucked away in a small drawer. On a crumpled piece of paper were written the words of Isaiah, the prophet: "Thou wilt keep him in perfect peace, whose mind is stayed on Thee, because he trusteth in Thee." (Isaiah 26:3).

My friend had found the gift of the untroubled mind as the result of a new and vital relationship with God. He rejoiced in Christian fellowship and had himself become strong by lifting the burdens of others. Above all else, he had learned the meaning of Christian love and the unutterable peace that it brings.

Those who have found that peace know it as a gift the world can neither give nor take away.

Chapter 3

TO DRINK OR NOT TO DRINK

"And do not get drunk with wine . . . but be filled
with the Spirit."

(*Eph.* 5:18)

My FRIEND, Dr. Sidney A. Weston, had a unique and
helpful lecture he entitled, "To Drink or Not to Drink."
He would stand before a blackboard, chalk in hand,
when he addressed groups of young people on this
timely subject. Drawing a line down the center of the
board he would proceed to list the arguments pro and
con.

At first one squirmed rather uneasily as the reasons
for drinking were listed: the wide acceptance of the
custom; the entree it affords in certain social circles;
the so-called "harmlessness" of drinking in moderation;
the exultant feeling of exhilaration and relaxation.

But soon the arguments began to pile up on the other
side of the chalk line. We will not list them at this point.
Suffice to say that before the talk was over, the evidence
against the use of alcoholic beverages was overwhelm-
ing. Many a youth upon leaving the meeting would say,
"I guess I'll leave the stuff alone." The point is that these

youngsters had not listened to a condemnatory harangue on the subject of drinking; instead, they had listened to a calm and objective presentation of a timely subject, had seen the arguments marshaled, and, in the light of them, had dared to make their own decisions.

After making a scientific and medical study of alcoholism in the United States, Drs. Merrill Moore and Mildred G. Gray of Harvard described their findings as revealing "a great chronic emergency."

Surely, we can no longer be casual on so critical a subject. It knocks at our very door. It taxes our spiritual ingenuity. It beggars research. In the end, we must all make a decision one way or the other. What is more, our Christian and democratic heritage, won at such sacrifice, is at stake.

The plain fact is that we can dissipate that heritage. Edmund Burke was right: all that is necessary for evil to triumph in the world is for good men to do nothing.

A discussion of this kind necessarily deals with the presence, or the lack, of proper spiritual controls. It concerns the crucial place at which an individual, a home, or even a nation, rises or falls, endures or is destroyed.

In a highly imaginative article in the Washington *Post and Times Herald* of June 26, 1955, Alfred Friendly "projected" himself some several thousand light-years in space, for the purpose of reviewing the history of the planet earth. The writer imagines a committee of inquiry attempting to find a reason for the wholesale destruction of earth and the obliteration of earth-Man. That reason was to be found *not* in a lack of spiritual and intellectual enlightenment or in a lack of moral ideals. Rather, it was grounded in something far deeper: in a lack of ethical and spiritual sensitivity and self-control.

A highly imaginative account of this kind is packed with a "wallop" for the simple reason that it might just possibly "happen." It is the time-lag between the massed physical power of our day, on the one hand, and the lack of ethical and spiritual controls on the other that has our scientific and spiritual leaders scared. The words of Frank Laubach come again to mind, as one thinks of our present world situation: "Grow up or blow up!"

In this chapter, we are dealing with but one facet of this immense "power problem." Statistics do not necessarily clinch an argument. They merely indicate a trend. And, yet, conservatively speaking, we have at least 60,000,000 social drinkers, 3,750,000 heavy drinkers, and 750,000 chronic alcoholics in our nation. "Cigarettes are now fully exposed to the X-ray of scientific research," said Paul Harvey in one of his columns recently. "The next major medical exposé will concern alcohol."

So let us not indulge in extended moralizing on the question we have set for ourselves. Let us face the fact that there was much in the "old approach" to the problem of drinking that time has rendered obsolete.

I speak out of my own experience as a pastor. In a former parish of mine, a pathetic procession of Saturday night alcoholics would crowd the minister's study to take the "pledge." These men would solemnly clutch the Cross and swear never again to take another drop. They didn't, that is, until the following week. Poor, bedraggled human nature, trying to make firm resolutions on its own strength!

Nor can the passing of a law or a statute solve our problem of national intemperance. It has become almost a cliché to say, "You can't legislate sobriety." What is needed is new research on this problem, research in which our best scientific, medical and religious minds join hands.

Meanwhile, let us look again at "the other side of the chalk line" and set down a few propositions, in the light of which each one of us must make up his (or her) own mind whether to "drink or not to drink." In the long run, each man's breast is the forum in which he must decide, and his own conscience must be his advocate.

I

Here is the first proposition: no man ever *drank* his way out of his troubles. Someone asked an Englishman why he drank so heavily. He replied that to do so was "the shortest way out of Manchester!"

Our age has been aptly described as an "aspirin age." A judge put it this way: "There is an increase in the use of drugs, narcotics, and opiates because people can't stand frustration. The people that come before me have no religion so they turn to the props of aspirin, drugs, and liquor. They can't take it."

Our generation suffers from a lack of nerve. Instead of facing up to the inevitable trials and temptations of life, we try to run away, to some kind of false escape, only to find that the short road out of our "Manchesters" turns out to be long. It's the "power problem" all over again facing us on the level of our personal lives.

> To every man there openeth
> A way, and ways, and a way,
> And the high soul climbs the high way,
> And the low soul gropes the low;
> And in between, on the misty flats,
> The rest drift to and fro. . . .[1]

Now the glory of the Christian faith lies in its realistic facing of the evils that beset men, whether uncertainty, fear, doubt, or the "low way." It commands us to look them all squarely in the face and, what is more, to look frankly and honestly into our own hearts. But the

[1] John Oxenham, "A High Way and a Low," *Quotable Poems* (Chicago: Willet, Clark and Colby, 1928), p. 7.

Gospel of Christ is not content with diagnosis—it is aglow with the positive offer of new and radiant life. Christ does not condemn men, He delivers men from the grip of vicious habit.

When Paul learns that there are Christian neophytes at Ephesus who are having a hard bout with their carnal appetites, he does not berate and scold them into a numbing discouragement. You do not stand on the safe bank and lecture a drowning man on the subject of lifesaving—you throw him a rope. Here are his words:

> Do not be foolish, but understand what the will of the Lord is. And do not get drunk with wine ... but be filled with the Spirit. ....   (*Eph.* 5:17, 18)

The great Christian gave them the same word that so many of us are needing now. "Throw away your false crutches. Stop leaning on false props. Dare to lean on God. Replace your false thirst with a true thirst for the things of the Spirit. This you *can* do, for Christ in you is the guarantee of victory." *That* is not only good religion—it is sound psychological procedure. Even an infant will not relinquish its toy unless you place something more attractive in its hands.

While cleaning the carburetor of my automobile on one occasion, a mechanic discovered that the gasoline had not been getting through to the motor and for a very obvious reason: there was no gasoline in the tank.

"Always keep your tank well filled," said the mechanic. "When the supply gets low, there is a tendency to suck in dirt and trash. When you drive into a gasoline station, say to the attendant, 'Fill her up!' "

There is but one reliable way to get rid of the emptiness that afflicts so many of our lives today; that is to fill them with something worth while: best of all, with the triumphant spirit of Jesus Christ. Replace the false habit with a good habit. Work *with* life rather than *against* life. Above all, watch the inner vacuum. "Be filled with the Spirit." ". . . where the Spirit of the Lord is, there is liberty." (II Cor. 3:17).

There was my friend Ray. He had become an alcoholic. After a long and bitter struggle with his temptation, he finally opened his heart to the message of a Salvation Army worker. He could not help noticing the gladness in her face, the note of victory in her voice, her sublime confidence in the power of Christ to deliver even an alcoholic. The close of that street service found my friend a different man. Let him tell us in his own words about the change that came over him: "Formerly, I could not seem to drag myself past the local tavern. Now Christ and I go by together."

II

We offer our second proposition: the easy counsel of *moderation* in drinking does not stand up in the strain and stress of modern life. It is a "pick-me-up" that turns out to be a "let-me-down." Approach any member of that remarkable organization, "Alcoholics Anonymous," and he will tell you, out of bitter personal experience, that total abstinence alone makes sense.

We do not suggest "moderation" in other departments of life's economy. For instance, which of us would say to a beginner, "Drive with moderate care on the highways of your city. Be careful up to a certain point." We know better. We hire an expert to teach our children how to drive safely. The life we save, when we exercise self-control behind the wheel of a high-powered car, may be our own.

Safe living, in our highly mechanized day, is a matter of pin-point precision requiring the co-operation of all. We engage the services of a trained dietitian to see that our food is safe and well balanced. We demand absolute sobriety of the surgeon who operates on our loved one in the hospital, of the educator who instructs our child in the schoolroom, of the minister who stands in the pulpit of our church, of the dentist with his hand on the drill. In all these departments of modern life, we simply will not tolerate immoderation. The reason is not far to seek.

Dr. Henry W. Newman, of the Stanford University Medical School, has this to say: One ounce of alcohol retards muscular reaction 17.4 per cent; increases time required to make a decision 9.7 per cent; increases errors due to lack of muscular coordination 59.7 per cent.

Mind you—just one ounce! That single ounce can wreck the economy of daily living and cost lives.

Small wonder that the American Orthopsychiatric Association gave half of its annual meeting in 1955 to the study of alcoholism. Not only the man in the pulpit but the doctor, the psychiatrist, the engineer, the businessman, to name only a few, are proclaiming the sanity of total abstinence.

III

Our third proposition: no one needs to be a "social drinker" in order to attain worthwhile popularity or success in life. No more so, it might be added, than it is necessary to be profane in order to be emphatic.

I am not advocating a wishy-washy, negative kind of goodness that reckons righteousness by its abstention from the things that others do. Heaven deliver us from the man—or woman—who is forever "sniffing out" his friends and associates for evidence of some newly acquired sin!

We need a robust and enthusiastic kind of goodness at work in the world today; a kind of goodness that will work like a cleansing leaven in a society that is morally run down at the heels. As Dr. Harry Emerson Fosdick has said, we need to regain the fine art of making goodness attractive.

A small boy, after attending Sunday School for the first time, was asked for his impressions. "I like it fine," he said. "It's much more fun learning to be a Christian than it is going to the devil!"

The American Businessmen's Research Foundation, after engaging in considerable study, came up with the conclusion that beverage alcohol and business do not mix well. This foundation went on to list the conclusions to which scientific discoveries have led. These, briefly, are fourfold: (1) alcohol is a narcotic; (2) alcohol is a heart-depressant, always, and a deterrent of every normal bodily function; (3) alcohol is a habit-forming drug; (4) alcohol is a dehydrating protoplasmic poison. "We condemn 'drinking driving' as well as 'drunken driving,'" so concludes the report.

That does not mean that *all* professional and businessmen of the nation are total abstainers. It does indicate, however, that an increasing number of men—and women—of the world of practical affairs are growing impatient with the cheap exhibitionism they see on every hand and are earnestly striving for a renaissance of clean and wholesome living.

The newly elected officers of a service club decided to install a bar at their place of meeting. For a time it was tolerated. Then, without any lengthy discussion of the propriety of the innovation, the plan was quietly abandoned, largely out of respect for one member of the club whose spirit of self-denial and whose sterling character were admired by all.

The truth is, we do not need to lower our ideals to be well thought of. What reflective person among us but has been utterly bored by the average run of a cocktail party and the half-witted performance that accompanies it!

A rather pathetic letter, written by a high school girl recently appeared in a daily newspaper. This youngster was visibly embarrassed whenever she attended social functions with her mother. What could she do, she asked, to make her mother realize what a dunce she made out of herself at cocktail parties?

To American youth we say: the best time and the most fun are still to be found in the companionship of people who practice the old-fashioned virtues of self-denial and self control. Listen, for instance, to these words:

> . . . Addressing one another in psalms and hymns and spiritual songs, singing and making melody to the Lord with all your heart, always and for everything giving thanks in the name of our Lord Jesus Christ to God the Father. (*Eph.* 5:19, 20).

Does *that* sound like a pink tea party? Or like the morbid ravings of a society of prudes? Hardly. The most lasting joys are to be found wherever God's people meet together in the spirit of the Apostolic *koinonia* (fellowship).

Dr. Halford Luccock tells of the good-natured policeman who stopped him in New Haven city traffic and asked, "What is the degree which many preachers have which makes them doctors?" The reply, "It is usually a D.D." The face of the officer lit up. "Why," said he, "that is the commonest entry on every police station blotter in the country, 'D.D.' It means 'Drunk and Disorderly.' " Dr. Luccock says that as soon as he was safely out of traffic he began to think of what the genial officer of the law had said. Sure enough, over there in the exciting pages of the Acts of the Apostles, officials threatened to arrest the disciples on the charge that they were "drunk and disorderly." "They are filled with new wine," so the authorities charged. And disorderly? Yes, indeed. For wherever these spiritually intoxicated men went, they turned the world upside down. Dr. Luccock, distinguished teacher of young seminarians, adds that he would like to confer the sublime degree of "Drunk and Disorderly" on all aspirants to the Christian ministry! "Far too much modern Christianity," says Dr. Leslie Weatherhead, "is floated on afternoon tea parties." It has gone tepid and colorless. We modern churchmen would do well to become "drunk" with the Spirit!

IV

This discussion of ours has one more proposition both pungent and personal. We had better admit, with ancient Cain, that we *are* our brother's keeper. Over a Christian doorway are inscribed these words: "Be careful of the kind of life you live. You may be the only bible some people read."

Actually, there is no mistaking the matter. Our lives and our personal example "preach"—and preach out loud.

Many a father has had radically to revise his sense of spiritual values because of a little fellow who insisted on walking in his footsteps. In fact, many social cancers that now afflict our human society will begin to disappear when enough of us have the courage honestly to live the religion we profess. The challenge to that kind of high and noble living comes ringing down the centuries. "For once you were darkness, but now you are light in the Lord; walk as children of the light." (Eph. 5:8)

A hard headed businessman of my acquaintance told how he arrived at the decision to abandon the sale of alcoholic beverages. In his own words, he "followed home" the product that was sold at his own counters. He got a close-up of the human misery that stems from indulgence in drink: poverty, wretchedness, broken homes and marriages; in fact, all the tragedy that follows when men are tempted above their power to resist. Any minister, social worker, doctor, or nurse could have told him long before. At any rate, what he saw at firsthand persuaded him to forego profit for the sake of self-respect.

Those who have attended summer conferences at Star Island, a few miles from historic Portsmouth, New Hampshire, will remember a beautiful custom observed at the close of each day. Just as the moon was rimming over the world, a procession with lighted lanterns would quietly make its way up the stony pathway to a little chapel. Upon entering the chapel, each person would hang his lantern on the wall.

It is when we let our lights shine in obedience to the command of Jesus that we help dispel the darkness of the world. Surely, the moral of the story need not be pressed. No pale policy of neutralism will do in the intense moral warfare abroad in our land. Jesus commands us to let our lights shine that men may see our good works, and glorify God.

Look around you today. Look within yourself and listen to your own heart. Look above yourself to the example of the most radiant and sacrificial life that was ever lived. What is His will for you?

"To drink or not to drink?" You must decide!

Chapter 4

HOW SHALL WE THINK OF
OUR DEPARTED ONES?

"He is not God of the dead but of the living."

(*Mark* 12:27)

ON JULY 7, 1951, a man by the name of Fred Sanders of Belvidere, New Jersey, lay on an operating table. He was undergoing a routine operation at Warren Hospital, Phillipsburg, New Jersey, when an amazing thing happened. His heart suddenly stopped beating and for a full five minutes he was "dead." The surgeon, Dr. Homer Bloom, realizing what had happened, cut open Sanders' chest and massaged the failing heart with his hands. Gradually the heart began to beat again. After five minutes of "death," Fred Sanders lived.

Ever since that unique and exciting experience, Sanders has found life a greater adventure than it formerly was. He humbly acknowledges that a Supreme Power restored him to life on that crucial day in the operating room. Indeed, all of life has become different!

The little things that once got him down no longer bother him. Formerly he would fuss and worry about his job. No more of that. There is no evidence that he saw things in that "other world" which were hidden from him here. He is just grateful to God and glad to be alive. The fear of death is gone—for good.

But what of our loved ones who have left our midst? How shall we think of those whom "we have loved long since and lost awhile?" Sooner or later that question must come to all of us.

Here in our church in St. Petersburg, Florida, we hold a monthly "Question and Answer" night. All kinds of questions are submitted. One that is perennial in interest is the one we are now considering.

A woman who regularly listens to our Saturday night broadcast asked that I visit her in the hospital. She had recently been bereaved of her husband. Now as she lay on her bed convalescing, she had time to think of the many years of happiness they had shared together. She believed firmly in the Christian teaching of the immortality of the soul. Now that her husband had preceded her in death, she did not know how to think of him. In God's good time they would be reunited in terms of a larger and higher kind of existence. But *how* to think of him meanwhile puzzled her. A great Frenchman is reported to have said, "I regret that in my heart I let the dead die."

If an attitude of evasiveness is to be deplored when

it comes to the ultimate issues of life and death, so also is the attitude of know-it-all. There are the pretentious individuals who need the sobering rebuke of Dr. Reinhold Niebuhr, that when it comes to a knowledge of heaven and hell, it is best *not* to pretend to know all about the furniture of the one or the temperature of the other! Perhaps we can *be* something to our friends in their time of bereavement instead of saying something.

Little Mary made a sympathetic call on a friend who had lost her mother. Asked what she had said, upon her return, she replied: "I didn't say anything; I just put my arm around her and held her close." She had expressed the highest type of sympathy. She had been to another soul "a cup of strength in some great agony."

Let us return again to the woman in the hospital. Here are a few suggestions that seemed to help her as we talked together that evening. Let me share them with you in the hope that they may be of some help when you think of the friend or loved-one no longer by your side but still in your heart.

I

First, think of your dear one as being very much alive. Those who have loved and served God during their earthly sojourn go right on living and moving and having their being in Him, the Eternal.

Perhaps you noticed the words of Scripture which head this chapter. They are the living, vibrant words of Jesus. They were addressed to the skeptical Sadducees who came to do some dialectical word-fencing with the Master. What an impossible picture they present to Him! A woman, in turn, had seven husbands, all of them brothers. In the heavenly state, which one of these seven brothers should she acknowledge as her rightful mate? Instead of tilting verbal windmills with His questioners and holding the discussion on their level, see what Jesus does: He lifts it to a higher altitude, so high that they could hardly follow Him with their stuffy and earth-bound reasoning. "Get off your low and groveling plane of life!" He says, in effect, to the Sadducees: "In the higher life of the Spirit, people are no longer given in marriage. The trammels of the earthly state no longer apply to them. They are free spirits. What is more, you do not know the great Father of spirits: He is not God of the dead, but of the living." As my wise friend, Rufus Moseley used to say, with a grin, "Jesus never conducted funerals, he conducted resurrections."

When I want knowledge and guidance in the things of the Spirit—about God, the soul, destiny, judgment, eternal life—I go directly to Jesus Christ. He knew both worlds, intimately—this one and the next. From God He came and to God He returned. When Mary and Martha grieve over the death of their brother Lazarus,

He does not speak empty platitudes. (What foolish things we sometimes say to our grieving friends, when a reverent and discreet silence is best!) Instead of using empty words of "comfort" and "sympathy," Jesus lifts the sisters' minds into the atmosphere of the spiritual. He makes it clear that He Himself is "resurrection and life," and that those who really live and believe in Him never die. Jesus not only demonstrates this eternal life in Himself but restores Lazarus to life in this world.

We poor humans lack eyes for the invisible! We are so "cribbed, cabined, and confined" within the sphere of the senses that we forget that, now and here, we "live and move and have our being" in God. We are poor practitioners of immortality. And so the dear ones who precede us in the experience of death seem at times very far away. But be of good cheer; Jesus is here to remind us that we have a *living* God, and that because He is the Father of living spirits, "all live unto him."

There are some words of Phillips Brooks which have always been an inspiration to me. He was seeking to dispel the gloom and darkness of unbelief and skepticism from the lives of his hearers. He wanted them to know that their departed ones live on in God. The great preacher said, "The world's poor heart knows very well what it wants. For years and years it longed to see one man rise from the dead. If it could only have that! It could let many other questions go unanswered, but, oh, for some light on *that* darkness—for some sound out of that silence!" Phillips Brooks concluded with words of buoyant faith: "No longer should spiritual philosophy labor under the burden of materialism; no longer should the dying die in terrible doubt, and the mourners go hopelessly about the streets. My friends, the world's prayer is answered. A true Man *has* risen from the grave! Life and immortality are brought to light!"[1] Lift the conch shell to your listening ears, and if you are attentive, you will hear the roar of the infinite ocean in it. Phillips Brooks echoed the reassuring words of Jesus: "God is God of the living." Our dear ones live in Him.

A woman once requested that I read James Whitcomb Riley's poem, *Away*, at a memorial service for her late husband. She wanted to carry the living image of her dear one about in her mind and heart. Her husband had been a man of kind and lovable disposition, and she wanted to remember him as she and his many friends had always known him. The lines of Riley helped to anchor that living image in her mind. They may do the same for us:

> I cannot say, and I will not say,
> That he is dead. He is just away.
> With a cheery smile, and a wave of the hand,
> He has wandered into an unknown land,

[1] Phillips Brooks, *Selections from the Writings of Phillips Brooks*, (New York, E. P. Dutton & Co., 1896), p. 108.

And left us dreaming how very fair
It needs must be since he lingers there.
And you—oh you, who the wildest yearn
For the old-time step and the glad return—
Think of him as faring on, as dear
In the love of there as the love of here.
Think of him still as the same, I say;
He is not dead—he is just away!

When one of their number passed away, we are told that the early Christians would accompany the body with songs and shouts of joy as though he were traveling to another place near by. They thought of their departed as alive in the living God. So may we think.

II

We should also think of our dear ones not only as alive but as expansive growing souls on a higher plane. What lives in God is never static, never stands still. When the beloved Rufus Moseley died, his friend Glenn Clark said of him, "Brother Rufus just graduated, that is all. He will be equally at home with the prophets of the Old Testament and the apostles of the New." Stop a moment and think: babies are dynamic little candidates for humanity. It is in their very nature to *grow*. There are the "seven ages of man," as Shakespeare characterized them. The great adventure of living is one of growth. Man is a creature of infinite potentiality, even in this world. Shall we not believe that those who have passed out of our mortal sight and graduated into the spiritual world continue the thrilling adventure of growth? That in God they still live and move and have their being? I believe that it is God's desire and plan to nurture souls to spiritual fruition all through eternity.

Unfortunately, there are those who have made heaven very unattractive through their weird excursions into Scripture. They have taken portions of the Bible and quoted them without rightful regard for the full context. As a result, they have come up with false and morbid pictures of heaven. In fact, their ideas of the afterlife are so dismal and strange that no sane man would care for it.

I have a lot of sympathy with the little boy who was continually being reminded by his mother that he would not get to heaven unless he behaved better. Finally, one day the little chap asked, "Mother, if I do go to heaven, will it be quite all right if I have a little devil up from hell to play with me, once in a while?" In view of some of the unlovely caricatures of the beatific state that you have encountered, do you blame that boy?

Now Jesus never gave His disciples long and intimate details concerning the life to come. There is no exhaustive blueprint of heaven in the New Testament. A sublime reticence characterizes the Master when He speaks of the heavenly life. For instance, He says, "I have yet many things to say to you—many sublime secrets to whisper into your hearts—but you cannot bear them now."

Nowhere in the teachings of Jesus do you find any suggestion that heaven is a Dantean inferno out of which the spirits of the departed must be "prayed." Nor does He picture it as some dismal Sheol in which the spirits of just men, made perfect, aimlessly wander. Instead, he refers to heaven as "My Father's House," a spacious and infinite abode, in which there are many, many rooms, way-stations, "mansions"; that life, freed from the trammels of flesh and blood, and the limitations of time and space. is to be an adventure in terms of infinite being:

> Hope that can never die,
> Effort and expectation and desire,
> And something evermore about to be.[2]

I remember John, my esteemed and elderly minister-friend, who said that he believed that God would have something for him to do in eternity. Pearly gates and angelic harps just would not be enough. The best was yet to be!

[2] William Wordsworth, "Prelude."

"In my Father's House," says Jesus—and in that House there will be work to do, souls to love, and tasks to be completed. Shall we not dare to believe it? As Dr. E. Stanley Jones has said: "It is too good *not* to be true."

III

We need to think of our departed ones as retaining their individual identity in the life beyond.

A friend of mine was present, many years ago, when Dr. S. Parkes Cadman was beginning his broadcasts from the Brooklyn YMCA. At the close of his message, the famous preacher had time for questions. On this particular day, a gold-star mother asked the question, "Will I know my boy in heaven, even as I have known him here?" We are told that Dr. Cadman fixed his great eyes on that sorrowing mother and said, "Woman, you will know your son." The words were spoken with a conviction that carried away all doubt and wavering uncertainty.

The Good News that sounded out from an open tomb, in that early Mediterranean world, was of two-fold significance: first, that Jesus, Himself, had survived the ordeal of death. The risen Christ revealed Himself to chosen witnesses after His resurrection in a personal manner. There, in the Upper Room, where He is re-united with His disciples, He is *not* a wraith or disembodied ghost but the dear personal friend who has sat at table with them and often fished with them on Galilee's waters. "It is I, myself, handle me and see," he tells them. (Luke 24:39).

Secondly, He who had conquered death shares the gift of eternal life with His disciples. There is little comfort for most of us in a vague belief in the absorption of souls into an abstract infinite. Also, mere talk about the "immortality of influence" is of small help to a mother grieving over the loss of her child, or a wife over her husband. Nor are we "begging" the question when we reason in this manner concerning the great adventure of death. No. On the contrary, we long to be reunited with loved ones and friends because we have learned the secret of love in this life. In loving unselfishly, we have shared the very nature of God. "We love Him— and one another—because He first loved us."

Moreover, if, as Jesus taught, God is the infinite and eternal Father of spirits, then God's own character is at stake in this whole matter. He loves, cherishes, and preserves His children, as persons, distinct identities. Our heavenly Father has plans for us far beyond this little space-time continuum we call the world. He has embarked us upon a career of infinite consequence. In the cross of His son, He has redeemed us unto himself, at great cost. And, no more than we human parents would think of scrapping the lives of our children at some crucial point in their development as persons, will God toss us "to the void," at the last.

How beautifully Emerson states this trust in thinking of his own child:

> . . . . What is excellent,
> As God loves, is permanent;
> Hearts are dust, heart's loves remain,
> Heart's love will meet thee again.·

IV

Let me suggest one more thing. Try thinking of your departed ones not as far away but as close beside you in the hard battle of everyday living. Think of them as close by you when you are on your knees seeking God's will for your life. A man of my acquaintance derives great comfort and help from the practice of including his wife, who has preceded him in death, in his prayers. As he prays, he feels her near, and the great love of God enfolds them both. And why not —if God is the Father of living spirits?

Believe me, this way of thinking is not an opiate to dull the feelings and make life grimly bearable! Far from it! It is a summons for us to "lift up the groping hands and strengthen the weak knees" (Heb. 12:12), to dry the saddened eyes, and to go forward with Christ in unselfish service for God and fellowmen.

My dear wife, late by my side, loved and served the church, had a tender heart for the welfare of little children, and was deeply concerned for the progress of God's Kingdom on earth. Then, rather than sit and grieve, let me give myself with a renewed sense of devotion to the cause which was so dear to Him—and to her.

There is a face, the strong face of a man, that comes to me as I write these lines. He was one of those rare souls you can never forget. He had arrived at the heyday of his life when he was informed that a serious disease would soon lay him low. With a short time to live he made the minutes and the hours and the days count. No murmur of complaint ever escaped his lips.

First, he set his own spiritual house in order. He felt he must be worthy of the great gift of eternal life. Any misunderstandings that he might have had with others along the way were cleared up. And how he cheered those on who bore the brunt of the burden, in their homes, in their church, and in their community! He came to understand, more deeply, the meaning of the words, "Buy the truth and sell it not," and "Let us redeem the time, for the days are evil." When, finally our friend passed from our midst, there were no "mourners" at his funeral. Those who were present said that they could feel his living spirit present. He was one who could affirm with Walt Whitman:

> My foothold is tenoned and mortised in granite,
> And I laugh at what you call dissolution,
> And I know the amplitude of time.

Let us then think of our dear ones as *alive*, as *growing*, as *retaining their precious identity*, as *close by our side*. We sorrow not as those who have no hope.

Jesus has taught us faith in a living God and Father. The mask has been stripped from the face of death. Our loved ones abide in Him.

Chapter 5

I STILL BELIEVE IN PEOPLE!

"Letters for Christ, written not with ink, but with the spirit of the living God."

(*II Cor.* 3:2)

THERE is a delightful story of an old Quaker who was in the habit of sitting on a bench in a quiet square in the center of the little township where he lived. A new-comer addressed him one day, saying, "What kind of people live here?" The old Quaker replied, "What kind of people didst thee live amongst before?" "Oh, they were mean and narrow and suspicious," answered the stranger. "Then," said the Quaker, "I'm sorry, but thee wilt find the same manner of people here."

Sometime later another newcomer sat beside him on the bench and asked the same question, and, like his predecessor, was asked, "What manner of people didst thou live amongst before?" "Ah, friend," said the visitor, "never did I live among such fine people. They were generous, kind, and loving. How I did hate to leave them." The old Quaker eagerly reached out his hand and said, "Welcome, neighbor, thee wilt find the same people here." That may be an old story but it bears repetition in our day. We have developed a passion for debunking and debasing human nature.

A paymistress employed in a large factory used to say that the men who crowded up to her window for their pay envelopes reminded her of nothing so much as a herd of swine! We have lost faith in men, if not in man. The august meaning of the words of the book of Genesis needs to dawn on our minds with fresh significance: "Then the Lord God formed man of dust from the ground, and breathed into his nostrils the breath of life; and man became a living soul." (Gen. 2:7, R.S.V.). Not just an intelligent brute or a soulless automaton, but a living soul, bearing the image and the superscription of the eternal on the inner coin of his being. *That*, and nothing less than that, is man!

In these days of blurred vision, let us dare to grasp again the great central truth of our Christian faith and gospel, that God became man in Christ, that man might become godlike. Therein lies the meaning of the Christian doctrine of the incarnation. God Himself has entered the stream of our humanity. Christ has intimately shared our human frailties, sins and sorrows. Beware, therefore, what label you pin on this creature, Man.

Count Leo Tolstoy was once accosted by a beggar asking for a coin. The great Russian reached deep into his pockets but could find nothing. "Alas, my brother," he said, "I have nothing to give you." The beggar replied in memorable words, "You have given me something far more precious than money; you called me 'brother.'"

That noble company of elect and gracious souls, the "Friends," have a belief which they take seriously when they say that *"there is that of God in every man."* Actually, we see in others a reflection of that which is uppermost in ourselves. What we need right now is to get our sights raised. If the depth psychology has dredged up the seamier side of man's nature, there is nevertheless a splendor concealed in him. His dust is mixed with divinity.

In his *Essay on Man*, Alexander Pope makes the famous statement that "the proper study of mankind is man," and then goes on to say:

> Created half to rise, and half to fall;
> Great lord of all things, yet a prey to all,
> Sole judge of truth, in endless error hurled;
> The glory, jest, and riddle of the world!

Ah, but there is so much more to be said. That man who walks beside you on your way to work, or sits by you in the tram car, is a child of the living God. He is, as George Buttrick has said, "a creature born for a revelation."

A scene out of my boyhood home comes vividly to mind. A disgruntled church member called at our home and proceeded to find fault with another member of the flock. No word of opprobrium was spared in the condemnation. After he had finished speaking, my wise and gracious Christian mother spoke: "In spite of all that you have said about this man, he is still God's child, His image and likeness, and that's that."

For my part, I shall go right on believing in people. I agree wholeheartedly with Halford Luccock:

> We have had enough dictator's-eye views of man, in which he appears insignificant and devoid of rights and dignity. We now need a God's eye view of man, in which he has a supreme and undebatable worth.[1]

A young college professor friend of mine, frankly disappointed in his dealings with human nature, once engaged in argument with his pastor. He cynically remarked, that to his knowledge, no one any longer believed that human beings could be changed. The reply he received shattered his cocksureness and helped to straighten out his thinking: "Jesus does." The argument was unanswerable. Jesus knew what was in man and needed not that anyone should tell him. That, however, is not the whole of the matter. Jesus "actualized potentialities" within men. He took this sorry, bedraggled thing called human nature and made it over into the stuff of divine sonship!

[1] Halford Luccock, *Treasury of the Christian Faith* (New York, Assoc. Press).

I Still Believe In People!

Living as he did, in the crude and callous world of the first century, A.D., Paul got a close-up of raw human nature. Like his Master, he knew what was in men. In his missionary travels, he suffered unspeakable indignities, slights and insults. But with the new eyes which Christ gave him, Paul saw human nature in an entirely different light. "You are a letter from Christ," he wrote the converts at Corinth, "written, not with ink, but with the Spirit of the living God." (II Cor. 3:3 R.S.V.).

What a compliment to pay the former enemies of the cause of Christ, so recently lifted out of paganism! This is not humanism, with man at the center; nor romanticism, with its doctrine of automatic progress. This is Christian faith looking at man as a Michelangelo looked upon his crude block of marble and seeing an angel concealed within.

Let us make four definite assertions about human nature.

I

Human beings are capable of *loyalty*. When you are tempted to despair of human nature, bear in mind what the Almighty has been able to do with plain, ordinary mortals like ourselves.

When the glory of their divine sonship dawned upon the first Christians, they could not refrain from exclaiming, "Thou hast made us kings and priests unto our God!" Made extraordinary through the power of Christ, they laid the foundations of a Christian conception and way of life. They built eternity into time. Womanhood was redeemed from its low estate. Little children became sacred. The first glimmerings of the Christian home and commonwealth appeared. Peter, James and John, and others of that first circle of the redeemed had looked upon the world through the eyes of Jesus. And now, all men, however unpromising they might appear to others, were to them the potential sons and daughters of God.

These newly redeemed men and women were people of intense loyalty. They were willing to lay down life and limb for the Lord who had given them spiritual birth. One of them even dared to write, "We Christians hold the world together." (*Epistle to Diognetus*).

Nor is that kind of moral chivalry by any means extinct in the world today. When headlines depress and you become fed up with human nature, think back over your life and call to memory the names of persons who have given you a lift along the way. Believe me, you will find this to be effective therapy.

I remember hearing a minister of mature years call out the names of individuals who had been a help to him in his work. What would we ever do without the loyalty of the great anonymous fellowship of those who are willing to stand for the hard right against the easy wrong in this topsy-turvy world! You say you find people fickle, unreliable? "Not I," says Paul, and he points to the churches he has founded, where those who have felt the transforming touch of Christ were joined together in mutual love and fidelity. You might find them in communities scattered all over that early Mediterranean world: little colonies of heaven, holding the world together. Christ had made living exciting for them!

A fellow pastor has a fitting reply for the occasional cynic who disdainfully refuses to have anything to do with the church because, as he says, "there are too many hypocrites in its membership." "Come right in," my friend replies, "there is always room for one more!"

II

Human beings are also capable of *courage*. True, that quality is not always in evidence. But to deny that it is there, deep in the inner reservoir of men's souls, is simply to overlook the facts. Many of us who have observed human nature at close range, through the years, are ready to share the grand optimism of Robert Browning:

> Oh, we are sunk enough, God knows! but not
> quite so sunk that moments
> Sure, though seldom, are denied us, when the
> spirit's true endowments,
> Stand out plainly from its false ones.

Living Can Be Exciting

On the surface, we humans sometimes appear to be a rather shabby and shoddy lot. But deep within us there is what Napoleon called a "three o'clock in the morning courage," which rises up to meet the emergencies of life when they come. When Winston Churchill offered the British people the option of "blood, sweat, and tears," they rose up as one to meet the challenge. Regardless of the right and wrong of war, we, here in America, can only witness to the gallant response of youth when their country called.

I believe that we make a mistake when we tone down and soft-pedal the appeal of the Christian religion. A merely "air-conditioned" and Cross-less religion is a travesty, as well as an affront, to intelligent people. A watered-down, invertebrate version of historic Christianity is deserving only of contempt. No wonder that millions of the world's youth have trailed after false and vicious messiahs! Good respectable church people like ourselves have failed to offer the stern, uncompromising religion of the Son of Man.

There comes to mind a weekly church advertisement which appears in a prominent newspaper with its reiterated appeal to softness. In large letters appear the words, "Elevator—no stairs to climb." What a far cry from the sturdy appeal of One who called on men to deny themselves, take up their cross daily, and follow Him, if necessary even to the death! Maltbie Babcock used to say that Jesus offered only three things to those who dared follow him: they would find themselves filled with a deep peace, they would be ridiculously happy, and they would get into trouble.

III

Human beings are also capable of *compassion*. Again, the evidence at times seems far to seek. We have only to read our morning newspapers with their dismal account of crime, pettiness, and misdemeanors, to say, "What a *lowly* creature is man!"

Our juvenile crime statistics are enough to bring the blush of shame to our cheeks, that is, if we are still capable of blushing.

Our contemporary society often resembles an antheap with men trampling over each other in a frantic effort to get ahead. "Man's inhumanity to man which makes countless thousands mourn," so George Romanes referred to our human predicament.

The important thing is to keep a sense of proportion in our thinking about human nature. We are not trying to make black appear white. Human beings, sometimes even "good people," can be cruel, calculating, and cunning—the exact opposite of compassion. We can make our religion into a cloak of hypocrisy, our politics a means of besmirching and defrauding the characters of innocent people.

And yet I, for one, shall go right on believing that

the great majority of my fellow citizens honestly strive to live decent and God-fearing lives; that they are inherently kind, considerate, and compassionate. The devil still gets the headlines while fidelity and goodness are relayed to the back page, if mentioned at all.

Even as recently as Nov. 7, 1954, Martha M. Elliott, Chief of the United States Children's Bureau, wrote in the New York *Times* that 95 per cent of American youth are not delinquent. The great majority of adults and youth of our land still hold with Robert Louis Stevenson that there is an ultimate decency at the heart of things.

After girdling the globe as a newspaper reporter, David Loth tells why he believes in the basic integrity of the human heart:

> I believe in people. However much of a mess we seem to make of this world, it is people who have brought about all the progress we know, and I don't mean just material progress. . . . I would rather trust my own experience and observation than the cynical remarks of unhappy men—the lesson of history—is that people's instincts are most always right. You can trust them.[2]

In the church I serve, we have a weekly radio program. Every now and then we make an appeal in behalf of some worthy cause—the plight of Korean children, for instance. Almost invariably the response is gener-

[2] Edward Murrow. *This I Believe*, p. 103.

ous. You find yourself exclaiming how innately kind and generous is the human heart! You become aware that the Good Samaritan still lives; that underneath a cold and forbidding exterior there often beats a warm and generous heart.

IV

But if human beings are capable of loyalty, courage, and compassion, they are also capable of *aspiration*. I believe that God created man with a spire on his soul.

"The soul," said Tertullian, "is naturally Christian"; and there is, as Calvin wrote, "a sense of the Deity inscribed in every heart." It is that irrefutable truth about ourselves that makes living exciting in such a world as ours. Once let us cease to aspire and we cease to be men.

Daniel Evans, whom I mentioned in an earlier chapter, tells of the elevating effect the humble but God-fearing lives of Welsh miners had upon his boyhood. Their religion was a felt reality and power in their lives. It revealed itself in their daily vocation and in the crises that came to them. They trudged the earth but they walked with God. They loved the house of the Lord and walked far to reach it. They listened with rapt attention as the Word of God was read from the Bible and proclaimed from the pulpit of their plain churches. Simple, devout, God-fearing—*such* were these humble folk.

Out of their midst arose a breaker-boy of the mines by the name of Daniel Evans to say, "I felt I must become a minister."

Man at his best—and after all that *is* man—is a dreamer of dreams. In our generation we have lived to see two of these dreams at least partially realized. The first is the World Council of Churches, which William Temple pronounced the greatest single fact of our time. The other is the creation of the United Nations which, like the World Council of Churches, has a notable record of achievement. Behold what God hath wrought through men and women who dared to listen to His voice and obey His will!

Despite the social pessimism of our day, the human spiral is upward. In the prophetic words of Tennyson, the race as a whole has dared to:

> Move upward, working out the beast
> And let the ape and tiger die.[3]

Speaking at the tenth anniversary of the founding of the United Nations at Los Angeles, President Eisenhower said among other things that peace "cannot be a mere stifling of guns. It must be a glorious way of life. In that life, the atom, once dedicated as man's slayer, will become his most productive servant."

Let us dare to believe with Emerson that Jesus alone saw the greatness of the human soul and endeavor to

[3] Alfred Tennyson, "In Memoriam."

look again at ourselves and at our world through His anointed eyes. God give us the imaginative insight and daring of a Paul that we may claim the unchristianized of our day as "letters for Christ."

When enough of us do so, the much longed for new day will have dawned!

Chapter 6

GO INTO THE SILENCE AND LISTEN!

"And after the fire a still small voice."

(*I Kings* 19:12)

A FRIEND of mine found himself in a mental and physical quandary. He had driven himself hard for years to make his niche in life. But now the structure of his life seemed to be rapidly crumbling. The vital enginery of mind and body appeared to be worn out. If he held to his present pace, he would soon find himself upon the human scrap heap. The inevitable rest cure was prescribed and gloomily accepted.

Fortunately, he found himself out in the country where hills and valleys, trees and flowers could minister to him: where the "boundless scheme" of nature could work upon his tired and troubled faculties. A new world swam into his ken. Above all else, he learned again to be quiet. In that quiet, he looked from nature to "nature's God," and felt the healing of God's Spirit. He learned his lesson as so many of us must sooner or later learn it—the hard way. In the hectic rush and press of modern living, we must take time to be still, and, in the stillness, to listen for a Voice and to quest for a Presence.

When Elijah, prophet of God, stood upon the mount of Horeb, spent, fearful and depleted, ready to give up, it was in the silence that healing and renewal came to him. After the earthquake, wind and fire had wrought their havoc and made their ominous sound, there came a "still small voice" like the breath of a gentle whisper. And being "tuned in," as he was, the prophet discerned the voice of God in that gentle whisper, speaking to him, encouraging him, giving him a new sense of direction, and girding him with a new sense of mission, until, strong and resolute, he again took up the burden of life.

John Greenleaf Whittier was a man who knew the wisdom and the joy of entering the silence, finding it dynamic and alive with spiritual meaning. His biographer, W. Sloane Kennedy, tells us how Whittier loved nature as the handiwork of God, and how, with her myriad voices, she held him enthralled: "To their songs [the birds] and to the murmurs of the tall pines by his window, he listens, then looks into his heart and writes." [1]

This is the man who translated the experience of the prophet into the immortal lines of a great hymn, so that

[1] W. Sloane Kennedy, *John Greenleaf Whittier* (Boston, B. B. Russell, 1892), p. 154.

generations to come might stand upon the mount of vision and listen and commune and be healed.

> Drop thy still dews of quietness,
> Till all our strivings cease;
> Take from our souls the strain and stress,
> And let our ordered lives confess
> The beauty of thy peace.

Let us look, now, at just a few of the many facets of that silence.

I

More than anywhere else, we see this silence epitomized in Jesus, "the great silent Man," as Carlyle called him.

When a Chinese convert was asked his opinion of the Christian religion, he replied by saying, "Well, it's a very talkative religion!" The point of view was well taken. So often we substitute talk for earnest endeavor, verbosity for the travail of solid thinking.

What is more, we generally think of Jesus primarily as a "preacher," as one who spoke words. And such He was. His words on occasion could be almost frightening, as when He uttered blistering "woes" to men He considered to be pretenders in religion. Or, consider that sermon He preached in His own home town of Nazareth, challenging the smug complacency and provincialism of His townsfolk, and ending His sermon with those trumpet-toned words: "This day is the Scripture fulfilled in your ears!" No one crowded around the preacher at the close of that service to say, "I enjoyed your sermon." Instead, they thrust Him from their presence as though He were a criminal and would have destroyed Him. They feared Him because "His word was . . . with power."

Nevertheless, our Lord was primarily a *man of silence*. He knew, as did none other, that there is a time to speak and a time to keep silent. If we, who would serve him in our day, would learn the secret of His winged and penetrating utterance, we must see Him at his night-long prayer-vigil on some secluded mountain top, alone, in silent communion with the Father. In Him we behold:

> The silence of eternity,
> Interpreted by love.

Sustained and intense seasons of silence were the inevitable prelude to the great crises in His life. Before He chose the twelve who were to be with him and share His ministry; before He gave that sermon which has been the spiritual blueprint for the progress of our race; before He faced the trial and the cross—Jesus knelt in silence, and listened, and was divinely empowered. He has left us an example that we might follow in His steps.

After gently chiding us for being so verbally effusive and spiritually ineffective, Thomas à Kempis gives us one of his most beautiful sayings about needful silence:

Blest is the soul that hears its Lord's voice speaking within it,
And takes the word of comfort from his lips.
Blest are the ears that catch the throbbing whisper of the Lord,
And turn not to the buzzings of the passing world——
And blest are they who try to give their time to God,
And shake them free from all the burden of the world.

II

The lack of the discipline of creative silence in our lives reveals itself in our lost capacity to carry on a meaningful conversation with others. The old-fashioned art of conversation, in which there was the spirit of mutual give and take, has almost disappeared. We rarely pay each other the courtesy and respect of hearing the other person out! Instead of engaging in an orderly process of mutually shared thought and conviction, we toss mere driblets of ourselves into an incoherent and jumbled mass we dignify by the name of "conversation."

Into our childhood home there would occasionally enter a garrulous neighbor. Once seated, she would let go a torrent of speech which covered national events, neighborhood gossip, and the latest happenings at the village church. It was a solo flight. Under ordinary circumstances, our mother could hold her own, but not against this adversary! After talking herself—and her unfortunate victims—into a state of sheer weariness, this good woman would invariably rise and bid us adieu with the words, "I enjoyed our 'conversation' so much!" She was the epitome of your modern tandem talker. What she actually wanted was not a charmed circle in which to share thought and information but a dictaphone into which to pour an endless monologue.

> I am Sir Oracle,
> When'er I 'ope my mouth
> Let no dog bark.

A "talkathon," however interesting, is a sorry substitute for sincere and shared conversation. There is something *you* really want to say to *me*—something fine, noble, and worthwhile—and I must afford you the opportunity of saying it.

The slave philosopher, Epictetus, insisted that the fact that we were created with two ears and one mouth is proof positive that we should listen twice as much as we speak. Sad, indeed, that we moderns have it in reverse.

Our only right to speak lies in the fact that, first of all, we have listened.

Those of us who are engaged in some phase of Christian work owe an incalculable debt to the late Richard C. Cabot. This great "Olympian" knew how to be quiet, how to listen respectfully to the opinions of others, and how to express himself in simple and direct speech. He made it a special point to teach his students that patient, creative *listening* to others in their trials and troubles was powerful therapy and would often, by itself, produce the miracle of healing.

How often we have seen this wise counsel of Dr. Cabot come true in the years since. How often persons have unburdened themselves of inner tensions and guilt feelings while we sat by and patiently listened. Often the counselee has said, "Thank you so much for helping me." And all we did was to listen.

Let us learn again the art of meaningful conversation.

III

There is need for us to enter the silence and listen in order that we might also find healing for the many hurts of life.

The increasing mechanization of our modern culture and the intense specialization in education have tended to produce a race of mass men who need to recover the dimension of *wholeness* in living.

To add confusion to the scene there is the constant, relentless hammering of the modern radio and television with their mass conditioning of the minds of children.

Go Into The Silence And Listen!

Because my wife and I have been ardent devotees of Henry David Thoreau and his teaching of simplicity in living, we made our way to Walden Pond during one vacation. We expected to find many pilgrims on reverent tiptoe at this shrine. What we actually found was people picnicking all over the place, their radios blaring out a loud cacophony. Hardly a soul seemed acquainted with the rich lore of the place. The name of Thoreau fell on deaf ears.

Thus do we convert our shrines into "Coney Islands" of confusion. The modern pulse is jittery, noisy, and confused.

In the instance of Elijah at Mount Horeb, it was after the prophet entered into the spirit of a composed silence that the Eternal spoke to him, comforted and counseled him, and set him on his feet. Up to that point, Elijah had done most, if not all, of the talking.

Our services of divine worship must provide more opportunity for the creative and reverent use of silence. There should be extended intervals where the burdened soul communes with the Unseen through no other medium than that of silence.

In our church, we have experimented with this medium of worship, particularly at our Wednesday evening service. At first there was the inevitable and expected awkwardness—a dead-pan quietness, a vacuum in which nothing much happened. But gradually the interval of silent meditation and listening has been lengthened, with resultant blessing and benefit. Worshipers have found help and healing for agitated and disturbed mental states.

George Fox, famous Quaker and great practitioner of the discipline of quiet waiting upon God, counseled his followers to relinquish their agitated and intense frame of mind and gradually to rise up through silence into the very thought of the Highest; until, as Longfellow has said, "God alone speaks in us."

Someone has said that our minds often resemble a glass of turbid water which needs to stand quietly until the accumulated sediment sinks to the bottom. So in the discipline of silent waiting upon, and adoration of, God, we need to let the earthquake, wind, and fire spend themselves until, like Elijah, we stand exultant and wonder-eyed upon the mount of vision.

A neophyte who attended a Quaker meeting was visibly perplexed at the long and extended period of quiet which prevailed. Turning to a fellow worshiper, he asked when the service would begin. "The service begins," came the eloquent reply, "after the hour of worship is over."

One of my richest memories stems from the early days of seminary training at the old Bishop Seabury Mission at Faribault, Minnesota. At an early hour of the day, students and faculty would file into the oratory, in complete silence, and kneel at the altar. As they knelt, taut nerves were relaxed, purposes were clarified, motives purified, until a new splendor from on High shone on their faces.

"All the troubles of life come upon us," said Pascal, "because we refuse to sit quietly for a while each day in our rooms." Martin Luther translated the words of Psalm forty-six, "Be still and know that I am God," as follows: "Be thou silent unto God and let him mold thee."

If we humans did as much—if we experimented only a little with the great discipline of silence—new peace and power would well up within us.

IV

All that we have said thus far might possibly be interpreted as being selfish except that, across the roar and tumult of the world's unrest, God waits to speak in the/summons of that voice which communicates itself to those who will listen.

"Statesmanship," said Gladstone, "is finding out where God Almighty is going in the next seventy-five years, and then going in that direction." Few will deny that the greatest need of our day is for quiet and "collected" men who have discovered the will of God in the stillness and have had the breath of God's Spirit wafted upon their minds and hearts—inspired men through whom the Eternal can accomplish His purpose in the world. It was after he had stood upon the mount of vision that Elijah went out from the presence of the Lord to overturn false kingdoms and to do the impossible.

We need a surcease from cheap and vicious demagoguery in our day, deliverance from endless harangue and bitter debate. The earthquake, wind and fire of human stupidity and folly have wrought their havoc. In a world where the lash of communism and the upsurgence of suppressed peoples are making themselves felt, there is a yearning for the leadership of a genuine Christian statesmanship. We need not only the knowledge of God for our time but the moral courage to act. Where else shall we find them than upon our knees, before the God of righteousness, justice, and mercy? God waits to speak His word of deliverance and healing. Will we have the grace to hear it?

Those who visit the Meditation Room of the United Nations will come upon a little pamphlet. It is entitled, *A Call To Prayer*, and has been prepared by friends of the Meditation Room for U. N. delegates and peoples of the world. On one page is a picture of a man, quite likely a delegate, kneeling in simple reverence at an altar. His head is resting in his hands as he humbly seeks the will of God for his life. Underneath the picture is inscribed an eloquent plea for a revival of prayer as "a catalytic power providing a constructive atmosphere where divergent human minds can find solutions beneficial to all." Study the picture and the words and the conviction is borne in on you that the Kingdom of God will not come through human cleverness and power but as the statesmen and peoples of the world listen for the word of God and obey it. Now, as ever, it is true that "the weapons of our warfare are not of the flesh, but mighty before God to the casting down of strongholds." (II Cor. 10:4, A.S.V.).

> Still stands thine ancient sacrifice,
> An humble and a contrite heart.

While attending a conference on international relations, the late Mohandas Gandi, famed Hindu leader, was, for a time, not to be found. The reason was known only to those who knew him. The great exponent of "soul-force" had quietly withdrawn himself from noise and confusion that he might keep inviolate his noon-day hour of prayer and meditation. The man to whom the millions of India looked for help and guidance knew where to turn for strength and inspiration.

Has living ceased to be exciting for you? Have the multiplied cares and troubles of the world gotten you down? Then enter into the silence and listen! The "still small voice" that spoke with such power to Elijah and to the Master will speak to you. It will lighten the burdens of your heart and make you a sympathetic and loving helper of your fellowmen. Best of all, it will enable you to look out upon a distracted world with new hope.

"And after the fire, a still small voice."

Chapter 7

HOW DOES ONE LEARN
TO HAVE FAITH?

"... If you have faith as a grain of mustard seed,
you will say to this mountain. 'Move hence to
yonder place,' and it will move."

(*Matt.* 17:20)

A FRIEND of mine overheard the following conversation at a bus stop one Sunday: "Did you have a good
service at your church today?" Reply: "Oh yes, except
for one thing." Question: "And what might that one
thing be?" Reply: "Why, it is just that so much that
our minister says goes over my head. He is everlastingly
telling us to have 'faith.' I would like to know how one
can get hold of faith. I know that Isaiah and Paul and
others had it. But how can I, an ordinary mortal, learn
to have it?"

When George Matheson went to his first church at
Innellan, Scotland, he experienced what seemed to be
a black-out of faith. Newly ordained to the Christian
ministry, he nevertheless found himself to be without

faith in God, immortality, or his own soul. The wise and gracious members of the Presbytery refused to accept their minister's resignation. They felt he was a young man and that he would change. He did. George Matheson not only lived through the darkness of those days, but eventually wrote the assuring words of the great hymn that bears his name and has strengthened the faith of so many, *O Love That Wilt Not Let Me Go*.

What happened between the flickering of the faith of the young minister and its renewal? What enabled him to trace again "the rainbow through the rain," and know that "the promise is not vain?" If we could know, we might be able to construct a chart and diagram of faith. But there is something elusive about great faith. There are no proxies in this vital business of believing. Each one of us must find his own way.

There has always been something deeply comforting for me in Jesus' words about the mustard seed and faith. After having so signally failed the father of the epileptic boy at the foot of the Mount of Transfiguration, the disciples come into the presence of their Master, discouraged and crestfallen. Why had they failed so miserably? Jesus tells them it was because of their unbelief. "If you have faith as a grain of *mustard seed*, you will say to this mountain, 'Move hence to yonder place,' and it will move; and nothing will be impossible to you." A mustard seed moving a mountain—it sounds preposterous, doesn't it? And yet, there, by their side, He stands, assuring them that, weaklings though they are, they can become strong men of faith.

Yes, I am glad that the greatest believer that ever lived used a mustard seed as the symbol of effective faith. George Washington Carver tells us that at one time in his life he asked the Creator to reveal to him the secrets of the universe. When no answer was forthcoming, he held up a humble little peanut, asking God to tell him about it. And the Lord said to him, "That is better, George; now we are getting down to your size!" The mystery locked up in the humble peanut opened up into vaster mysteries at the heart of the universe for the great scientist.

Jesus is telling us that the secret of great faith is buried in the heart of an unpretentious little mustard seed. A potential power is locked up within that tiny seedling that, once it germinates, can rend mountains. That humble little seed will grow into a plant so large that the birds of the air will come and build their nests in its branches. In His parable of the mustard seed, Jesus describes the nature of the very kingdom of heaven.

Living becomes exciting insofar as we lay hold on the explosive, energizing, miracle-working power of faith.

As learners within the great school of Jesus, let us consider a few of the guideposts that lead to that kind of faith.

Living Can Be Exciting

I

Suppose we begin with this: instead of being appalled and discouraged with your little thimbleful of faith, use what you have. Plant your little seed. Many of us have found that faith is much like the biceps on our arm; you must keep flexing your arm to make it strong. Small beginnings can have large endings. In a revealing statement about faith, William James once said:

> I am done with great things and big things, great institutions and big successes, and I am for those tiny, invisible, molecular, moral forces that work from individual to individual, creeping through the crannies of the world like soft rootlets, or like the capillary oozing of water, yet which, if you give them time, will rend the hardest monuments of men's pride.

There is a vine just outside my study window which has been a perpetual wonder to me. It seemed so frail and tender early in the spring that I was tempted to help it along. But that little vine proved to be a born climber. It turned its little tendril deliberately toward the sun and kept growing. Now I have to cut it back occasionally in self-defense. How much greater than a vine is a man!

William Adams Brown used to say that Christian faith is *not* believing a little in a lot of things but believ-

94

ing with all your heart in a few great things. For instance, a chaplain of the Second World War once told me that he had the least difficulty with boys who came from small rural churches, some of which were of the "holiness" type. These lads had moral stamina. Their intellectual grasp of their religion might not have been as sweeping as that of their more "liberal" buddies, but they possessed a few elemental convictions which enabled them to parry the thrust of temptation. They believed that they belonged to Jesus Christ, that body and soul were to be kept blameless before God, and that to sin was to incur penalty. I simply repeat what the chaplain said : "These were the lads who weathered temptation the best."

There is a vital difference between the faith of tradition and the faith of conviction, as the great preacher, Phillips Brooks, used to say. There is a hand-me-down faith which ends by letting you down. Such faith is the traditional belief of childhood, taken from other people, held because others have held it. But in the day of testing, the faith of mere tradition is not enough. The belief which brings salvation and inner victory is the vital faith of conviction in which God speaks directly to the heart.

An old peasant was observed sitting silently and alone in a church, his eyes intent on a crucifix on the altar. Asked what he was doing, he replied: "I am looking at Him, and He is looking at me." In this vital

confrontation and in this living encounter, saving faith
is born.

Perhaps the question we should ask ourselves is *not*:
"How can I have more faith?" but "Am I using what I
have?" Vital life-giving faith is much more than intellectual assent to a creedal proposition. "You can repeat
the entire creed," said Phillips Brooks, "and yet be an
atheist at heart." In the words of Horatius Bonar:

> Great truths are greatly won. Not found by
>   chance,
> Nor wafted on the breath of summer dream,
> But grasped in the great struggle of the soul,
> Hard buffeting with adverse wind and stream;
>
> And in the day of conflict, fear and grief,
> When the strong hand of God, put forth in
>   might,
> Ploughs up the subsoil of the stagnant heart
> And brings the imprisoned truth-seed to the
>   light . . .
>
> Truth springs like harvest from the well-
>   ploughed field,
> And the soul feels it has not wept in vain.

That kind of faith seldom comes easily. Faith of that
kind is venture—the vital venture of the entire man,
with the consent of all his faculties, toward all of God
that he knows. "Dynamic whole-response," Nelse F.
S. Ferre calls it.

Don't neglect the mustard seed because of its small-
ness. Plant it. Use what you have. Faith grows stronger
in the using.

II

Let us go a step farther. Once that vital spark of
faith is kindled in a man, he goes right on believing, all
outward appearances to the contrary. Over the door of
his college in London, Charles Haddon Spurgeon had
inscribed the words, "I hold, and I am held." It is that
way with Biblical Christian faith.

> Now faith means putting our full confidence in the
> things we hope for; it means being certain of things
> we cannot see. It was this kind of faith that won their
> reputation for the saints of old.
>
> *(Hebrews* 11:1, 2,
> J. B. Phillips' translation)

There is a story that Spurgeon went one day to visit
a farmer who was a member of his church. On a wind-
mill on the farm were written the words, GOD IS
LOVE. "Do you mean," asked the great preacher, "that
your faith in God is dependent on the direction the
wind is blowing?" "No," said the farmer, "the words
mean that, regardless of which way the wind blows,
God is love."

Living Can Be Exciting

In his poem, *Lincoln, the Man of the People*, Edwin Markham has a fine line about his hero:

> He held the ridgepole up and spiked again
> The rafters of the Home. He held his place—
> Held the long purpose like a growing tree—
> Held on through blame and faltered not at praise.

That is the sterling faith we need in America today, faith that will hold the "ridgepole up" in a difficult hour. The times are "out of joint" and have gotten us down. Faith has flickered into fatalism. The spiritual atmosphere is overcast with the fog of doubt, fear, and suspicion. We seem to be more sure of what we are *against* than of what we are *for*. We look with pessimistic eyes at our children's and our nation's future. Like those first disciples of Jesus, spiritually impotent in the face of desperate need, we lack strength to cast out fear, hatred, and suspicion. When we are no longer sure of God, we begin to point the accusing finger at one another. The demon of cynicism blights everything it touches.

Dr. Elton Trueblood insists that the most damning sin of the modern church lies not in its divisions but in its moral insipidity. Living in a time of crisis when a dynamic fellowship is needed to turn the world upside down, we are offered a stereotype. A man goes to church hungry for bread and is forced to "sing sentimental songs with words he does not mean, listen to some comforting platitudes, and finally shake the minister's hand at the door, because there is no other way of escape!"[1]

Emerson was right: the great ages were the ages of dynamic, positive faith. The most menacing disease of this present day is the disease of little faith.

I dare to believe, however, that underneath this exterior of blighting cynicism and unbelief there still burns the vital flame of faith. We haven't quite thrown the baby out with the bath! Call to mind the man who, upon leaving a church, was overheard to exclaim, "I'm an atheist, thank God!" Even atheism presupposes something to be denied. As many of our American men stated upon their return from World War II, there are few atheists in foxholes.

Stern and revolutionary times like ours can be great times for faith, shaking us loose from cheap and deceptive escapism and bracing us afresh to "hold the ridgepole up," both for ourselves and those who are to follow us. The eleventh chapter of the Epistle to the Hebrews fairly bristles with that militant faith. Let us get our eyes off our own little fears and foibles and set them on the great heroes of the race as they are pictured in this chapter: strong, poised, and fearless in a time of terror. After the hard battle of faith is fought and won, no easy prizes are put into the hands of the winners. Rather do we read, "And all these, though well attested

[1] Elton Trueblood, *Alternative To Futility* (Harper), p. 43.

You can be a ridgepole in god's church

by their faith, did not receive what was promised, since God had foreseen something better for us, that apart from us they should not be made perfect." (Hebrews 11:39, 40, R.S.V.). That is holding the ridgepole up!

Think of Robert and Mary Moffat working and praying for over ten years in the Bechuana mission without a single convert. Their friends wrote beseeching them to forsake the poor heathen and return to civilization. Instead of heeding that counsel of cowardice, Mary Moffat asked her friends to send a Communion set. "Send us a Communion service; it will be needed."

In the year 1829 a great spiritual awakening swept the mission. The thanksgiving of converts and the singing of hymns sounded out from that formerly pagan mission. The Communion set arrived just in time. Faith and patience had won their reward. That kind of faith is not only held by the believer—it holds him. "I hold, and I am held."

Tennyson describes it in *The Ancient Sage*:

> She sees the Best that glimmers thro' the Worst,
> She feels the sun is hid but for a night,
> She spies the summer thro' the winter bud,
> She tastes the fruit before the blossom fails,
> She hears the lark within the songless egg,
> She finds the fountain where they wail'd "Mirage!"

III

Ultimately, however, vibrant creative faith of the kind we have been describing is based not on what men can do but on God's power. Such faith hews out channels through which the Almighty can work. It becomes a cooperative endeavor in which God can use us to accomplish his purposes in creation, history, and redemption. When Morrison decided to give his life as a Christian missionary in China, his acquaintances chided him. "So you think you can make Christians out of those heathen?" Quietly Morrison answered them, "No, I don't think that I can; but I believe God will." God and man working together, and God *using* surrendered and obedient men to his glory and for the furtherance of his Kingdom on earth—that is the manner in which a living faith functions.

Martin Luther used to say that even a humble straw, lying flat on the surface of the waters, can feel the boundless power of the ocean surging through it.

Meaning and purpose and joy enter our lives when we know ourselves to be harnessed to the majestic purposes of God. We become channels of the very life of God to our fellowmen. A miracle-element enters into faith at this point in our spiritual growth. Things get done by means of a power beyond ourselves. Said Matthew Arnold, "God is that power, not ourselves,

LINCOLN BIBLE INSTITUTE

that makes for righteousness." Anxiety, needless fussing, and fear go out of our lives and a new serenity takes their place. Quietly, and with assurance, we plant our little mustard seed of faith, do all we humanly can to ensure its growth, and then trust in God for the outcome. Faith has invisible allies.

A humble farmer plants his crop and then waits patiently and trustingly for the sun and dews and rain to do their part. The farmer has invisible allies in nature.

The wise physician says, "I dress the wound, God heals it."

The more astute minds among our scientists are also humble. A friend listened as Sir Arthur Compton taught his Sunday School class. The famous scientist told his students that in every discovery he ever made he "gambled" that the truth was *there*, and then acted in faith until he could "prove" its existence. The scientist's discovery became God's revelation.

The greatest Christian worker of all time, the Apostle Paul, gives us the secret of the success of his immense labors for the Kingdom. "I planted," Paul says, "Apollos watered, but God gave the growth." (I Cor. 3:6 R.S.V.). He can do the impossible through Christ who empowers him. He rests back on God.

Even the Son of God, whom we have described as the greatest believer that ever lived, depended upon that other One to accomplish His vast benefits for mankind. "The Son can do nothing of himself but what he seeth the Father do: for what things soever he doeth, these also doeth the Son likewise." (John 5:19).

You and I can know the infinitely sustaining power of the Highest in our daily lives. We can know it when some great burden comes pressing in on us and the world seems to be crashing all around us. At such times we feel like boats, stranded on a sandy beach, waiting for the tide of God's power to come in and rescue us. Many of us, in our greater hours, have discovered the strength we needed.

While waiting for an elevator in a large city hospital one afternoon, I saw a man in a wheel chair. A mutual smile began a friendly conversation. This man had barely survived a tragic accident. His spine had been painfully injured and many months would need to pass before he would regain the normal use of his limbs. Nor was that all. Three days after the accident he had lost his wife in death. A friend of the injured and bereaved man, who sat near by, made the statement that it seemed too much for one poor human being to bear.

I found myself repeating the words of an old Christian saint: "The Lord never lays more on a child of His than he can bear." "I know," said the man in the wheel chair, "I have found that to be true in my experience." I thought I saw a radiance suffuse a face that was lined with the marks of suffering.

To sum up: how does one learn faith? *Use what you have. Plant your grain of mustard seed. Faith grows with the using. When the storms of life come—hold the ridgepole up. And then, after you have done your best, rest back, in faith, upon the omnipotence of God.*

The voice still speaks to us down the centuries, "If you have faith as a grain of mustard seed, you will tell yonder mountain to move, and it shall move. And nothing shall be impossible to you."

Absolutely nothing!

Chapter 8

MAKE YOUR HANDICAP SERVE!

"... Will I rather glory in my infirmities, that
the power of Christ may rest upon me."

(II Cor. 12:9)

ONE of the finest statements ever made about anyone
was made by the biographer of Alice James. Alice
James, as you may know, was the sister of the famous
William and Henry James. She spent a great deal of her
life as an invalid. Here is the compliment her biographer
pays her: "She never accepted the horizon of invalidism." That is, her so-called handicap never penetrated
her soul; it never invaded her mind; she held herself
erect.

If the truth were known, *all of us* are saddled with
some kind of handicap, something that trips us up,
cramps our style, gets in our way. If it is not a physical
handicap—lameness of some sort, a prolonged illness—
then it is likely to be something psychological, some
kink in the mind, perhaps, that makes us say and do
things we later regret.

What matters in the long run is how we carry off our difficulties. For some years, I lived directly across from the Charles River in Boston, where I could see the beautiful tower of the Perkins Institute for the Blind. Occasionally, I had the rare privilege of providing a spiritual ministry for students in that school. The spirit of Helen Keller, its most famous alumna, fairly permeates that place. If anyone had occasion to complain of a handicap, it would certainly be this remarkable woman. At the age of eighteen months, she contracted a fever which left her both deaf and sightless; hence the problem of teaching her to speak was a difficult one. But just listen to her: "I thank God for my handicaps, for through them I have found myself, my work, and my God."

While still a boy in my father's church, I used to sit in wonder and admiration whenever I heard the name of Paul the Apostle mentioned. He carried off well a difficult handicap. There is no railing against life in any of his letters. We do not know just what his trial was. Some believe it to have been a defect in speech; others, malarial fever due to his long travels; still others, poor eyesight. And how he did pray to be rid of it! It seems quite certain, however, that all his life he was burdened with a handicap. But Paul learned to live well and fruitfully with his problem. In fact, he made it pay rich spiritual dividends. Just hear him say that he glories in his infirmity that the power of Christ may be released through him! "If I cannot be rid of it," he seems to say, "then I will accept it, dedicate it, glorify my heavenly Father with it." Actually, he *uses* it.

When our "thorns" and infirmities and handicaps threaten to discourage us, we can remember great souls like Helen Keller, Paul of Tarsus, and a multitude of others, both great and small.

We can call to mind,

> Milton the blind, who looked on paradise,
> Beethoven deaf, who heard vast harmonies;
> Byron the lame, who climbed towards Alpine skies;
> Who pleads a handicap remembering these?

Yes, who?

Walter Winchell, in one of his syndicated columns, comments on the fear and haunting doubts that annoy some famous stars of the entertainment world. Life is by no means all roses and success and adulation for them. Up there, behind the glare of the lights, are fear and frustration and a feeling of inferiority. What a ridiculous word, that word "glamor!" Here, for instance, was John Barrymore, a great triumph in a role, yet confiding to his brother the extent of his fears: "I'm scared, I hear thunder in the applause, a sign of storms to come." Don't envy the eminently successful in their various fields. They have their infirmities, too. But somehow, in spite of them, or even *because* of them, they have mounted to success.

But how may the average person turn his handicap to advantage? Is this really possible, or is it just poetic fancy? No, it is not. Let me tell you why.

I

First, rather than be defeated by them we can let our handicaps *throw us squarely on God for help and strength*. The sooner the false props come down in our lives, the better. We can become God-intoxicated souls. We can learn to revel in Omnipotence! We, too, can glory in our very infirmities so that heaven's strength may be revealed in us. If our physical equipment is faulty and meager, then we can become wealthy in terms of spiritual capital. Our weak point can, through the grace of God, become our strong point. "When I am weak, then am I strong!"

A lot of us still have to learn that secret of living. Instead of allowing our foibles and failures to throw us morbidly inward on ourselves, we can let them throw us directly on God for strength. The same holds true for those whom nature has endowed with a healthy and robust vitality. There comes a time when sheer physical strength is not enough. To lean on ourselves alone will no longer do. Until a man learns that, he builds his house on sand, and sooner or later, his little house of life will fall. And great will be the fall of it!

I remember a paralytic woman in one of my father's churches. She was remarkable in that she actually gloried in her infirmities! She used to play the violin at church and lead out with her vibrant voice in congregational singing. It was my privilege to wheel her down the aisle of the little church into the choir loft. Once there, she would take her instrument out of the case, tune it, and play the service prelude. She was an "exhibit A" when it came to making a handicap serve in the praise of God.

A committee of persons who were meeting together one evening in a church found themselves discussing the meaning of the Christian faith. Several who were present frankly admitted that they could not make much sense out of their religion. At best, it was an intellectual pursuit, a kind of rationale, to help them think things through—that was all. For still others, religion was an inner "hunch" that helped them over difficult places, something they could not define or explain. Meanwhile, another person in the room had quietly listened. This woman had a severe physical handicap and yet was regarded as the most effective member of that church. When asked her opinion, she simply said, "If it had not been for my faith in God, I would not be alive today."

Persons of this type, experimental Christians we might well call them, have done much more than simply "adjust" to a difficult situation. They have triumphed

over their obstacles by laying a firm hold on the resources of their faith. Not "compensation" but trans-
formation explains them. In Frank Laubach's fine
phrase, they make their lives channels for the revelation
of spiritual power. They are powerhouses of the Spirit.

II

Our handicaps can also impart to us a rare and beautiful fellow-feeling and *compassion for others* who know
firsthand the meaning of disappointment and suffering.
In the language of the Scriptures, we may be "baptized"
into a feeling for others' infirmities. That man working
close by your side may seem rather curt and gruff. He
may be someone who needs the gift of imaginative
sympathy and insight on your part. "Empathy," writes
John K. Lagemann, "is the ability to appreciate the
other person's feelings without yourself becoming so
emotionally involved that your judgment is affected."[1]
Even the Master of men had to learn obedience by the
things He suffered. A moment ago we mentioned Paul
the Apostle and his affliction. Hear now these beautiful
words of his: "Bear ye one another's burdens and so
fulfill the law of Christ."

When you stop to consider, the ones who can best

[1] John K. Lagemann, *Christian Century* (Feb. 23, 1955), p. 238.

help us over the hard hurdles of life are the ones who themselves have felt the pinch of need, the urge of temptation, the wear and tear of some long illness. Some of us have learned to love the beautiful poems of G. Studdert-Kennedy, famous chaplain of the First World War, affectionately known to his men as "Woodbine Willy." Wherever they suffered, sinned, or died, there he was by their side. On one occasion, a soldier came to him and with hot tears confessed a sin he had committed. Instead of scolding and upbraiding him, the great chaplain placed an arm of understanding around his man and said, "Son, I think I understand. That happens to be my temptation, too."

It was my good fortune to make the acquaintance of a semi-retired script writer of a well-known newspaper. Arthritis temporarily had laid her low. She came to the state of Florida where kindly sunshine gradually brought her a measure of health and strength again. Many a lesser person would have given up, but not she. She promptly entered into a relationship with a newspaper which brought her into intimate contact with other similarly handicapped persons. She would interview them, learning how they had made the most of their trials and afflictions. Then she would fling her hopeful words into print where those reading them could get a fresh hold on life. Well do I recall her, limping along slowly with the aid of a stick but spiritually and intellectually erect. Like Alice James, whom we mentioned before, she "never accepted the horizon of invalidism."

> I walked a mile with Pleasure, and she chatted all the way,
> But left me none the wiser for all she had to say.
> I walked a mile with Sorrow, and not a word said she.
> But Oh, the things I learned from her,
> When Sorrow walked with me! [2]

Once at a prayer meeting, I heard a man make a remarkable testimony. He told of the Christian compassion of his wife during the years when he was a derelict and an alcoholic. He did not mince words as he told of all the suffering and humiliation his sin had caused this good woman. Yet, through it all she never lost her faith in God and kept right on praying for his spiritual recovery. "I had no faith in God, myself," he said. "I had faith only in her faith. That brought me through."

It is a truism but one that bears repeating: it isn't so much what happens to us as how we *take it* that matters in the end.

III

Not only can our handicaps be the means of throwing us on God for help and strength and making us more sympathetic and understanding toward others. They

[2] Robert Browning Hamilton, *The Golden Book of Religious Verse.*

can also enable us to bring our very all and lay it on the altar of *Christian service*. I firmly believe with Ella Wheeler Wilcox:

> There is no chance, no destiny, no fate,
> Can circumvent or hinder or control
> The firm resolve of a determined soul."

*   *   *

> Gifts count for nothing; will alone is great;
> All things give way before it, soon or late.

Just stop and think of the souls we have mentioned: Helen Keller, the crippled violinist, the Apostle Paul, and the arthritic writer. All of them were impelled and driven forward, in spite of their handicaps, to make the most of opportunity, and to serve their fellowmen while they could.

Suppose that for the purpose of illustration we single out the greatest of them, Paul. He has only a few years remaining. He must make the most of them. Out he goes, revisiting the churches he had once founded, propping up the weak and wobbly believers, comforting the troubled and persecuted. Yes, on he goes, redeeming the lost through the Love which God has poured into his own heart and dictating those marvelous letters to an amanuensis so that they might comfort and inspire men through the ages. Forward he goes, saying, "I am willing to be spent and offered up!" What a way to carry off a handicap! What a manner in which to turn it into a triumph!

A few years ago newspaper accounts gave the story of a legless veteran returned from the war. He had a difficult time learning to use artificial limbs but finally succeeded. So splendid was his spirit that the Veterans Administration engaged him to make the round of various hospitals where similarly handicapped men were discouraged and beaten. Our hero had a way of visiting these men and saying, "See, I learned to do it, so can you." That, again, is making over a handicap into an advantage.

In the Florida community in which I live, we have many rare and gifted souls from all over the nation and abroad who worship with us. One of the most remarkable of them was an aged, retired Presbyterian minister. In spite of his many years, the fire of the Spirit still glowed within him. When he and his wife sat together in the church, their faces were radiant with spiritual love and light. This man knew firsthand the power of fervent prayer. He had a rare "concern" for the spiritual welfare of others. Some who read these words will consider their age as a handicap. Not so this nonagenarian! He would come into our church office, scoop up an armful of printed matter and go out into the streets of the city to distribute it.

One warm and sultry afternoon, I saw my friend at his work of distributing religious literature. I stopped my car and attempted to remonstrate with him. Surely, he should not be out doing this work on a hot afternoon in June! After all, he was a man ninety years of age and must look after himself! But all my efforts were in vain. He fixed me with a sharp look and proceeded to speak words which I hope I shall always remember. "Young man," he said, "when in his Word God says 'Go,' that means every one of us, including me." God's aged warrior believed that there were no "retired" Christians worthy of the name. He held that a man can witness for his Lord with his very handicap. And wherever he may be in God's great universe, he must still be busy broadcasting the Good News of Jesus Christ.

All of us have some kind of a handicap. What matters is what we make of it, how we carry it off. "Lives of great men all remind us we can make our lives sublime. . . ." Like the man of Tarsus, let us glory in our infirmities that the power of Christ may be revealed in us. God will help us to win that victory, if we will ask Him.

Chapter 9

SOMETIMES UP AND SOMETIMES DOWN

"When men are cast down, then thou shalt
say there is lifting up!"

(Job 22:29)

Ạ HIGH SCHOOL boy was sitting one day in the principal's office waiting for an interview. He had gotten into mischief and was bracing himself for the inevitable reprimand. As he sat waiting, his eyes caught sight of a calendar on the wall with a picture of a small boat beached on the sand. Relieving the desolateness of the scene were these words beneath the picture: "The tide always comes back."

That boy has long since grown into a mature and happy man. What is more, he has never forgotten the lesson of the picture.

In these rather difficult days in which we are living, it is well for us also to remember that *the tide always comes back.* The ocean of life seems to have gone out and left us stranded on misty flats. A consequent feeling of discouragement and letdown is the aftermath. The lines of the Negro spiritual aptly describe the mood of many in our day:

> I'm sometimes up and sometimes down,
> Oh yes, Lord!

I recently reread the Old Testament book of Job. It is great literature, to be sure. But far more than that, it is a dramatic portrayal of how a man can face the worst life can offer and come out still believing in the best. Usually we feel sorry for Job sitting there on his ash heap. All we treasure and value was filched from him: children, flocks and herds, and above all, the respect of one's wife. But see what he has *left*: his spiritual integrity and his equanimity of spirit, so that even in our day we speak of "the patience of Job." In the book of Job there appear these words: "When men are cast down, then thou shalt say, *there is lifting up.*" In the travail of his spirit, in the baffling variation of his moods, Job had something to hold him fast.

So may we. When the Ups and Downs of life come our way and we have the occasional and inevitable blue day, we should remember a few considerations.

I

Let us expect ups and downs rather than be surprised by them. Actually our variant moods are a godsend. None of us can stand on the dizzy heights of elation for too long at a time. In North Carolina there is a beautiful mountain top where our family delights to picnic, yet we would hardly want to live there.

Jesus took three of His closest disciples to a high mountain where He was transfigured before them. They heard Him speak intimately with great spiritual seers who had departed this life. Peter began in awed tones to talk of building tabernacles up there. But Jesus, with deep understanding and tenderness, took His disciples by the hand and lead them down again into the plain.

If a graph of the psyche could be drawn, there would be an occasional up-swing and down-swing. There would be the inevitable variation of moods known to us all. There would also be the horizontal line where our moods level off again. A merciful God has intended it so.

This variety of moods is present in nature. The rugged mountain peaks are tempered with the plains and the valleys. There are the nuances and gradations of creation—its ups and downs.

And so with ourselves! Let us never be disconsolate when "the dark night of the soul," as St. John of the Cross called it, comes our way. Bear in mind that you are in goodly company! The great saints had their "acidee"—their times of spiritual dryness and loneliness. Among them are Teresa, Henry Suso, John Bunyan, George Fox, and St. Paul. At times they found environment to be "a cruel cage, against whose bars the soul beats bloody wings, but all in vain." In this company may be found our beloved Lincoln, who knew days of deep spiritual desolation with God seeming far away. Sensitive souls have always felt this sense of acute depression the most keenly.

If we cannot always understand the mystery of our moods, we can at least endeavor to be understanding toward ourselves and others when these times come.

Dr. Daniel Evans, wise friend and teacher of theological students, had some good advice along these lines. When his students left him, the older man would always give this parting word of counsel: "And now remember, when it rains, let it rain."

That is common-sense counsel for us all. Do not be surprised at a querulous mood. Expect it. A friend whose even-temperedness I greatly admire told me that he thinks there is a little of the manic-depressive in all of us. The important thing to be borne in mind is that it will pass. As the wise court fool said to his gloomy sovereign, "This, too, shall pass away."

II

Again, do not feed the mood of discouragement with morbid self-pity. Above all else, get on with the business of living.

Living Can Be Exciting

A Negro hod carrier, so the story goes, sick of his job and weary of life, lamented audibly, as he started up the ladder with his bricks, that he wished he were dead. Another worker, high up in the building, overheard him and promptly obliged by dropping a load of bricks on his head. When the victim regained consciousness, his first words were, "Lord, I thought you could take a joke!"

When the off day comes, throw yourself with new abandon into the tasks of life. Know the restorative power of hard, honest work. Learn for yourself the truth of Michelangelo's words: "It is well with me only when I have my chisel in hand." Remember also the wisdom of Matthew Arnold:

> Tasks in hours of insight willed,
> Can be in hours of gloom fulfilled.

The fact is, most of us simply cannot afford the luxury of morbid introspection. Theodore Roosevelt, who cast such a spell over the imagination of the American people, was sickly and puny of physique early in life. He promptly subjected himself to a rigorous discipline for mind and body that made him both an example and an advocate of the "strenuous life." He believed that no man can be happy who is not at work.

A friend of mine intimately knew an old trooper in the entertainment world. On the afternoon preceding an appearance, he would say to the members of his company, "Now remember, take stock of your convictions, not your feelings. No matter how you feel, the show has to go on."

If left to whim and caprice, the economy of life would soon bog down. The essential work of life would never get done; this chapter would not have been written. Instead of attending church on a Sunday morning, we would be loitering at home reading a newspaper. Our children would not prepare daily school assignments, nor would mothers have meals ready on schedule. Yes, the show has to go on. Most, if not all, the rugged chores of daily living must be performed regardless of how we "feel."

> When duty whispers low, "Thou must,"
> The youth replies, "I can."

We need not only the discipline of "saving responsibilities" but a kind of activity that is creative and purposeful in nature. Many people today are fed up with mere free-lance living. In order to be spiritually and mentally healthy, we need a regimen of life that will bring order and meaning and discipline into the chaos that so often characterizes our lives. Suppose, then, that we try to outline a simple but effective regimen that can apply to all of us, regardless of age and circumstance. Here are a few things we *can* do:

We can begin each day by reading a few verses from

our Bibles. We can get God's marching orders for the day. We can let the great structural ideas of the Bible percolate through our consciousness. To have a mind occupied with great thoughts is to have a healthy mind.

We can begin the day with prayer, *prayer* that penetrates below the surface of things, probes the heart, and opens windows toward heaven. We can pray the prayer that surrenders our lives daily to God and to Jesus Christ. We can be a part of God's great army of intercessors throughout the world. I have known many a physically handicapped person to exert a wider influence for good than did others in full possession of their faculties. Prayer can make us workers "together with God." Spiritually speaking, the sky is the limit.

The Boy Scouts have a custom which we might well emulate—do at least one good deed daily. There is the kindly word that needs to be spoken, or the genial smile that can be beamed from the inner heart toward some troubled countenance. An elderly minister recently told me that he considered the best contribution of his long and fruitful ministry consisted in the letters he had written. He was an inspiring preacher; he had held many positions of honor. But the most helpful thing that he had done through the years (so he felt) lay in the little messages of hope and cheer he had sent to persons in their time of need. I can testify to the helpfulness of those letters of his, for I was the fortunate recipient of a number of them.

We can join, too, in the fellowship of praise and prayer and adoration. There is "lifting up" when God's people gather and sing out His praise and glory on the Lord's Day. A deaf man once told me that he rarely hears a word spoken at the service of worship but that he would not miss it for anything. Like John, on the lonely isle of Patmos, he is "in the spirit on the Lord's day" and is uplifted and helped. In the phrase from one of our great Christian creeds, he can say, "I believe in the Communion of Saints."

True, these are simple ministries: the Bible, prayer, the daily good deed, the worship of God. But they can be effective means of lifting drooping spirits God-ward for healing. We can know "lifting up" by becoming spiritually out-going.

III

Expect the occasional gray day. Don't cater to it but get on with the business of life. What else can we do? We can know that whatever happens, the soul and God endure. There is One who abides the ups and downs of our existence, the fickleness of our human moods. Be stayed upon Him. Dare to say with the Psalmist, "As the mountains are round about Jerusalem, so the Lord is round about them that fear Him, and delivereth them." Our Christian faith, says Dr. Whitehead, provides us with an object of devotion and loyalty that "stands beyond, behind, and within the passing flux of immediate things."[1] If it be my lot to dwell for a time in the Slough of Despond, or to pass through some valley of the shadow, then let me look up! Yonder are the hills.

Dr. John Sutherland Bonnell tells how, with a group of friends, he journeyed by rail from Geneva over into Chamonix, France. In vain the passengers looked from the windows in an effort to see the Alps. It was a cold, cloudy day and the prospect was depressing. Presently, as the train rounded a bend, the clouds lifted and the sun broke through. In the distance, plainly visible, towered Mont Blanc, over fifteen thousand feet above sea level, the snow lying like so many crystals upon its great bosom. It stood there as though to say, "I have been here all the time."

Dr. Merton S. Rice had a way of saying to discouraged people, "God is about."

Indeed, God is not only near but is waiting to bring us health and healing, if we will let Him. Dr. Albert Cliffe, radiant Canadian Christian, went to see a woman who had suffered much from nervous exhaustion and depression. She had prayed, over a long time, to be rid of her burden. All seemed to no avail. Subconsciously she had come to believe that it was God's will not to help her. But she was encouraged to believe that God

[1] Quoted by Georgia Harkness, *The Dark Night of the Soul*. p. 175.

willed only good for His creatures; that He would lift the burden of depression from her if she had faith to believe; what is more, that He was helping her *now*. As a result, her faith became an "operative" faith. Christ became a friend close at hand. She regained her hold on life. She became whole.

Did not the great Comforter say to His sorrowing disciples, "I will not leave you desolate, I will come to you." Jesus Christ gives us the "oil of joy for mourning and the garment of praise for the spirit of heaviness." In Him, as in none other, there is lifting up. "He turned our sunsets into sunrises" sang the first Christians. What He has done for many another in time of need, He will do for you and me.

In the beautiful words of Phillips Brooks:

> The little sharp vexations,
> And the briars, that catch and fret,
> Why not take them to the Helper,
> Who has never failed us yet?
>
> Tell Him about the heart-ache,
> And tell Him the longings too,
> And tell Him the baffled purpose,
> When we scarce knew what to do.
>
> Then leaving all our weakness,
> With the One, divinely strong
> Forget that we bore the burden,
> And carry away the song!

Chapter 10

DYING THE LITTLE DEATHS

"As dying, and behold we live!"

(*II Cor.* 6:9)

Ill. Colored Preacher
Casket — mirror

Ill.

NEWSPAPERS carried a most unusual story a few years ago: that of a man who attended his own funeral. No detail was overlooked by him in making arrangements. The minister, the undertaker, and the florist were all carefully prepared. Then, on the appointed day, he attended his own funeral.

Just imagine being a mourner at your own obsequies! We are not surprised that a lot of people quite frankly considered this man a little off center. Surely, no one in his right mind would do such a thing.

Nevertheless, there is a kind of sanity about a man's attending his own "funeral." We need to die the little deaths in order that we may live the "big life." Living is exciting because we are constantly dying and are constantly being reborn. In fact, we need to attend a whole series of funerals of our lesser selves! In the words of Frank Laubach, we may have "Christ-life [only] through self-death."

While in a strange city, a friend of mine dropped into a church for a noonday service. He almost threw himself into a pew from sheer weariness. Presently a man with fire in his soul entered the pulpit. For a time he spoke of the fear of death which holds many people subject to bondage all their lives long. Then, rather dramatically, he leaned forward, and, looking intently at his hearers, said: "My friends, why not do your dying *now*?" The sermon went on to tell of the lesser deaths that men must die. Only so could one enter the abundant life. My friend left the church that day with new enthusiasm for life. The old tattered remnant of a self was left behind—a new man walked out into the streets of the city.

The truth of the Christian gospel is best stated in the form of a paradox: *We live by dying*. Listen to the Apostle Paul, "I die daily." Says Tennyson in "*In Memoriam*": "That men may rise on stepping stones of their dead selves to higher things." Above all others hear the dynamic truth from the lips of him who is Lord of life: ". . . unless a grain of wheat falls into the earth and dies, it remains alone; but if it dies, it bears much fruit." (John 12:24). When Jesus said that, He was speaking of the death He himself would undergo in order that we might live. In this capacity to die to the old life lies the greatness of the human soul. As Emil Brunner has said:

> To believe means objectively to die—i.e., to die as that false ego which is identical with sin; and like-wise to believe means objectively to *rise again* as the new man—Christ in me. Faith, or rather life in the Holy Ghost, through faith, means a real participation in the coming world of the resurrection.[1]

good

Stated in the plain vernacular of the layman, this means that we have the sublime privilege of sloughing off the empty shells of our old selves so that we may live the vibrant, thrilling, new life which God has in store for us.

An ideal transcript of that life is to be found in the inspiring words of Paul: ". . . As unknown, and yet well known; as dying and behold we live; as punished and yet not killed; as sorrowful, yet always rejoicing; as poor, yet making many rich; as having nothing, and yet possessing everything." (II Cor. 6:9, 10—R.S.V.).

That "yet" is the bridge leading out of the "old" into the "new," out of death into life. That thrilling Good News can become alive in us.

Suppose that we look at a few of these creative mutations—these sublime doorways—opening upon the life abundant. Here are some of the little deaths we must die.

[1] Emil Brunner, *Eternal Hope* (Westminster Press). pp. 110, 111.

Dying The Little Deaths

First, there is the fundamental Christian experience known as conversion in which we die to self in order that we live for God.

If that glorious experience has been yours, you will remember with what doubts you once stood upon its threshold. Christ seemed such a hard bargainer. He not only asked for something: He asked for everything including your very self. And there you stood, hugging your little pantheon of false gods to your heart: worldly success, popularity, giddy pleasures, some secret sin. Yes, He asked for nothing less than a drastic alteration in your life.

And then, through the gift of faith, you dared to cut loose from the old moorings, to step out on God's promise. You left the old for the new. *You died in order to live.* You found Christ-life through self-death.

In her interesting book, *Everyman's Mission*, Dr. Rebecca Beard tells how she came into the joy of Christian living. A young woman "medic," her mind was conditioned by the materialistic teachings of science and humanistic philosophy. For a time her medical practice went along nicely. Gradually, however, her philosophy of self-sufficiency began to peter out. Her health gave way before the rigid demands of her calling. In her own words, she was "an intellectual snob of the first order," who was told by her medical associates to put her house in order and to get ready to die. Yet, as in many another instance, an inner voice whispered that she had another chance. Her salvation lay beyond human resources. In her own words:

> There was only one place to go and that was on my knees. I cried out, "What are you? Where are you? I don't even know what to call you, but come and talk to me. If you are there, help me. Either take me out of this or send me on."

Rebecca Beard, pushed way "out on the limb" of life through her utter helplessness, died in order to live again. The help came with abundant resource for living. She continues:

> And because my surrender was complete and my admission of failure absolute, there came a tremendous illumination of Reality. I saw my real self as always existent. . . . I went over the crest of the wave into another dimension. . . . Something of the lesser self within us must die, and the ego does not die easily in most of us.[2]

Rebecca Beard then subjected herself to a new spiritual regimen out of which there came an illuminated, vibrant, contagious self. Through her dedicated life

[2] Dr. Rebecca Beard, *Everyman's Mission* (Merrybrook Press, 1952), p. 60.

and helpful ministry she became a blessing to many others.

So it is when the Hound of Heaven bays at our heels and finally tracks us down! There is in all of us an inner nub of selfishness that needs to die. When the inner citadel surrenders and the larger life takes over, then a new self comes to the birth. The age-old discovery becomes our own: "For if a man is in Christ, he has become fresh and new." (II 5:17, J. B. Phillips translation).

II

There is another "death" that we need to die: that of a morbid anxiety about health of mind and body. It is a platitude by now that we live in an age of anxiety. The ills of the mind are often communicated to the body. Like the hypochondriac, we are continually feeling our pulse and suffer from what has been called "attention pains." Our ailments readily become the subject of conversation and the center of attention in the home.

A physician told me that at least 60 per cent of his patients' complaints have their origin in the mind. This morbid preoccupation with ourselves is another husk of the old self that needs to be sloughed off.

There is an elderly minister who has developed a

slight "murmur" of the heart. Every day of his life is a hard battle to fight, not only for himself but for his patient and long-suffering wife. The "murmur" has entered his mind and become the center of his life.

A new day dawns in our lives when, by an act of faith, we bring our many fears and anxieties, the many aches and pains of our bodies and minds, and lay them down on the altar of God. "Christ is the great Physician," said Dwight Moody, "no case can be too hard for him." If God does not see fit to remove our trials, He will give us grace to bear them with Christian fortitude.

While riding on a bus, Howard Whitman saw a woman reading her Bible. He asked her if she thought that her faith would spare her the hardships of life. "No," she replied, "but it will enable me to accept them."

We get a new lease on life when we learn to affirm health rather than illness, life instead of death, faith rather than fear. Jesus Christ can give us the *will to live*, in place of the will to die. Once you give yourself over to God, you are amazed to find how many others in the Fellowship of the Radiant serve Him with limited physical capital.

My friend and former college professor, Dr. Glenn Clark, used to have a morbid fear of high altitudes. He had developed a palpitation of the heart which held him in a constant state of anxiety. In his book *How To*

Find Health Through Prayer he describes his victory over this fear. It happened while he was speaking at the Rocky Mountain College YMCA and YWCA Conference at Estes Park, Colorado. Here he was 8,000 feet above sea level with his pet phobia. And then he had it out with himself—and God. The pattern of his deliverance was very much like that of Rebecca Beard and that of many others who have been similarly afflicted. Let him tell us about it:

> "You made me Father," I said. "I am more wonderfully made than any mountains. If you want to take me—take me. If you want to preserve me, you can easily preserve me. I leave it entirely to you. You decide it. I am your man." [3]

From that moment of complete commitment of himself, he began to get better. By the time he left Estes Park the palpitation was almost gone. His entire book is a thrilling account of a spiritual adventure in which a man learns to forget himself through prayer and the thrill of Christian service. Here, again, was one who found "Christ-life through self-death."

A woman who lived in constant fear of losing her mind was encouraged to believe that her mind was a part of God's mind. She was told to surrender herself fully to God and to rest in the assurance of His safe-

[3] Glenn Clark. *How To Find Health Through Prayer* (New York, Harper & Brothers, 1940), p. 29.

keeping. God could not lose His mind. Once her fear was replaced with a new and vital faith, she became completely well and was the means of bringing relief to others suffering from the same malady. She died in order to live.

On the wall of Chester Cathedral, England, are words which we should memorize:

> Give me a good digestion, Lord,
> And also something to digest;
> Give me a healthy body, Lord,
> With sense to keep it at its best.
> Give me a healthy mind, Good Lord,
> To keep the good and pure in sight,
> Which seeing sin, is not appalled,
> But finds a way to set it right.
> Give me a mind that is not bored,
> That does not whimper, whine, nor sigh;
> Don't let me worry overmuch
> About the fussy thing called "I".
> Give me a sense of humour, Lord,
> Give me the grace to see a joke,
> To get some pleasure out of life
> And pass it on to other folk.[4]

That little poem contains some homely counsel that could help us die another of the little deaths along the way: morbid fear and anxiety about our health.

[4] Quoted by E. Stanley Jones, *The Way To Power and Poise* (Abingdon-Cokesbury Press), p. 312.

III

But many others of us have never been converted at the point of our prejudices. We suffer from arrested spiritual growth and need nothing quite so much as to have our narrow horizons pushed out. We are racial and religious snobs, priding ourselves on our exclusiveness. We feel that we are "different" from people of another race, creed, or nationality.

The day arrives when we slough off that despicable proud self. Selfishness, hatred, callous indifference to the lot of others less fortunate than ourselves take to their heels. We join the human race. The Christian faith, with its teaching of the fatherhood of God and the brotherhood of all men in Christ, dawns on us with new meaning. The Christian ethic becomes something for us to live out in daily, concrete, human relationships. Like the newly redeemed Saul Kane in *The Everlasting Mercy*, we too can now say:

> I knew that God had given me birth
> To brother all the sons of earth.

Once a man is crucified on the cross of false and selfish pride, he finds that the teachings of the Bible, the creeds, and the hymns of the faith take on new meaning. They begin to speak to his "condition."

Living Can Be Exciting

A friend of mine told of seeing Jane Addams hold a little colored baby in her arms. There was a look of such love in her face that it helped him make his decision to enter the Christian ministry.

A mother was informed by a narrow-minded neighbor that her little son was playing with a "foreigner." That evening when her son returned from school, she asked him if it were true. "I don't know, Mother," said the little fellow, "I'll look tomorrow and then I'll let you know." The "color-blindness" and magnanimity of her boy deeply affected that mother. On her knees she experienced a new baptism of the spirit of love.

Dr. Frank Laubach is right: either we will "grow up or blow up!" Mature persons in positions of leadership and influence are needed more than anything else in this atomic age. If we can get enough of them—as Dr. Harry Overstreet has said—the world may yet be saved and the millennium of peace come. Life can be exciting just because we can die to our selfish and provincial little selves and learn with Robert Browning that "life is a chance at the prize o' learning to love."

You were once loath to let go of your son (or daughter) in marriage. But when you gave your loved one over in the spirit of trust and love, you held him (or her) all the more surely. That illness was the means not of destroying you but of discovering new inner spiritual resources. "What other significance can our existence have," writes John MacMurray, "than to be ourselves fully and completely?"[5]

Justice William Douglas says that when he sees people who are afraid to speak their honest convictions for fear of being thought unorthodox, or hanging on to their lives instead of throwing them away for the common good, he remembers the spirit of his pioneer father. Leaving for a hospital in a strange city to undergo serious surgery, he left these words with his family: "If I die, it will be glory. If I come through alive, it will be grace."

Whenever you find a man like that, you find someone who has died the little deaths that he may live the Big Life. He has found Christ-life through self-death. He has undergone crucifixion that he may know the power of resurrection. He has quietly slipped his hand into the hand of Another who still walks into the Galilees of tomorrow, asking the courageous to follow him.

To die to self, so that Christ can live His life in us; to die to the morbid fears of self-concern; to slough off the old provincialism that kept us from being a human being; to live a life of such trust in God and such love for our fellowmen that death itself shall be but translation into life eternal—*that* is to live.

"As dying, and behold we live!"

[5] Quoted by Karen Horney, *Our Inner Conflicts* (W. W. Norton), p. 183.

Chapter 11

STAND UP AND BE COUNTED!

"Joseph of Arimathea, a disciple of Jesus, but secretly ..."

(*John* 19:38)

A COMMITTEE of men met together to make a spiritual inventory of their church. What was holding it back from serving their community, nation and world more effectively? As the discussion proceeded, it became clear to these men that their church could hold its own in the usual resources of money, building equipment, membership, and social standing in the community.

Prayerful consideration brought out into the open what is at once the deepest need and greatest asset of any church: a spiritually regenerate and committed membership.

The strength of your church—any church—cannot be computed in terms of financial assets, social standing, or size of membership but in those invisible assets which defy calculation. The number of men and women within its ranks who are willing to stand up and be counted for Christ and church—these constitute its strength, its moral sinews.

When the building of the new Gothic chapel at the University of Chicago was first proposed, one member of the faculty held back. He would be willing to see such a chapel built, he said, providing there was some "Gothic religion" to put into it. Human societies, like individuals, must be spiritually arched and buttressed from within, lest they fall. And the Church of Jesus Christ, when it fails to be a transforming power at the heart of such a society, fails of its distinctive mission.

Far too many in our day are content to be nominal followers of the Christian Way. They are good people —but not good for much. Their names are inscribed on a membership roll but their hearts are not in the task. They resemble Joseph of Arimathea, who, on that first Good Friday, came belatedly to Pilate and requested the body of Jesus. There is a revealing note in the account which says that he was "a disciple of Jesus, but *secretly*, for fear of the Jews." He was a Christian, yes, but "on the Q. T." He never made open and public avowal of his love for his Lord. He wanted, as do so many of us, to soft pedal his convictions and play the game safely. Eventually, he came, after the shame and disgrace of the crucifixion, to offer post-mortem consolation. A phrase that was coined out of the Second World War describes him: "too little and too late."

We dare not be too critical of Joseph, however. At

least he saw to it that the body of Jesus received decent burial. But one thought refuses to down: what a power for good Joseph might have been if only he had made a public avowal of his discipleship. Post-mortems, however lovely, are shabby substitutes for loyalty in the heat of the battle.

> Where duty calls or danger,
> Be never wanting there.

We need to grasp the crucial importance of the role of the individual for our time. Absentee ownership, tremendous expansion in industry, and the presence of mechanical gadgets in our dwellings have not lessened it.

Herbert Agar would remind us that ours is "a time for greatness" and that we have yet to accept its challenge.

After mentioning the temptations to which Christian discipleship is liable in our day, the World Council of Churches, in its *Evanston Report*, said:

> In all these fields, the real dangers are complacency, lack of imagination, and the dull sense of hopelessness that settles upon those of little faith.

> (Report of Section III)

Stand Up And Be Counted!

The sense of hopelessness and little faith will vanish as we dare openly before the world to be disciples of Jesus Christ.

There are some inspiring lines in William Pierson Merrill's hymn that we do well to take to heart:

> Rise up O men of God,
> Be done with lesser things;
> Give heart and soul and mind and strength,
> To serve the King of kings.

I

One thing is certain. The rich blessings we enjoy as freemen in a free society were secured for us by men who were willing to stand up and be counted for their convictions. No pale policy of neutralism has brought us this far on our onward march. Our American forefathers were men of flaming convictions who dared to burn their bridges of retreat behind them.

When the *Mayflower* returned to the scattered little colony on Cape Cod, colonists were offered the opportunity of returning to their homeland. Not a single member of the Pilgrim band took advantage of the offer. The temptation must have been strong: persecution, suffering, hunger, and loneliness here; security, friends, and comfort in the mother country. But something unspeakably precious was at stake in this new adventure which they could not bring themselves to forsake. That intangible "something" is best stated in the words of the poet:

> Aye, call it holy ground,
> The soil where first they trod!
> They left unstained what there they found—
> Freedom to worship God.[1]

The Pilgrims knew a point of no return and they held to it for conscience' sake, whatever the future might hold.

Let your imagination usher you into the era of the first disciples of Jesus. Here were the first real pilgrims of history. Men like Peter, James, and John were recruited for the most part out of the more humble ranks of society. Nevertheless, they set the Cross over against the sophistry of the Greco-Roman world: the "might of the terrible meek" against the mailed fist of the Roman legions. At times, their remonstrance to the evils of their day must have appeared ridiculous. Christians were branded a "pestilential heresy" by the secular historian Josephus. They were a small, persecuted, and despised minority. However, they welcomed the opprobrium, threw themselves with abandon into the spiritual melee of their day, and nailed the banner of their faith to the door of Caesar's

---

[1] Alicia Heemans, "The Landing of the Pilgrims."

palace. As Dr. Carl Glover has said: "they 'out-lived, out-thought, and out-died' their pagan contemporaries."

But what, we ask, was the source of such sublime courage and conviction? It was the assurance that God Himself had spoken to the deepest needs of the human heart and that He had done so in the crucified and risen Jesus. It was the conviction, furthermore, that this same Jesus was Lord, not only of the human heart, but of history, and that of His Kingdom there should be no end.

There is a legend that the ancient Scots would throw the heart of their hero, Robert of Bruce, into the battle before them. The living and revered memory of their great hero made them invincible.

In some such way, we must try to account for the heroism of the first followers of Jesus. There could be no secrecy about their discipleship after the resurrection. The vivid sense of the living Christ was within them. They were inspired with a magnificent hope. We need to recall the Christian "greats" of history and take new courage for our day.

Remember John Knox praying, "O God, give me Scotland or I die!" He was more feared by "bloody Mary" than all the armies of Cromwell.

Remember Martin Luther on his knees saying, "O Thou my God, stand by me against all the world—Do Thou do it, Thou alone. It is indeed not my cause, but

Thine." He then stood alone and unafraid at the Diet of Worms.

Remember the Pilgrims entering into sacred compact in the cabin of the *Mayflower*, and, then, and not till then, embarking on a great new experiment on strange soil.

Make no mistake about it—the pathway of human progress is blood-splattered. It is not the numerical size of a people but their spirit that decides their destiny. When men are willing to stand up and be counted for Christ and the Kingdom, God enters with His redemptive purpose into history. The "impossible" becomes the possible.

II

When we ask, why has the sense of individual responsibility and Christian mission slackened in our day, the reasons are not easily stated. A complex of factors is involved, each making its own contribution and yet intermeshed with the others.

(1) For one thing, life has become so complicated in our modern impersonal society that individuals are often cowed into a feeling of inferiority. So fearful and so ominous is the power that has been unleashed that our "nuclear age" is an "age of anxiety." We feel a sense of bafflement before the vast complex of our

human problems. "After all," we ask, "what can one person do?"

We need to see again the strategic importance of the individual in our human society: that persons are still the focal center from which creativity proceeds; that human beings still initiate policy and are the chief motivating power in our world. In a word, we are not automatons but men with the stamp of the Creator upon us. . . .

A movement of our day which seeks to strengthen individual morale is known as the "Christophers." This fine organization teaches that it is better to light a candle than to curse the darkness. It stresses the importance of the individual in the righting of wrong. I may be only *one*, true, but if I am willing to do my duty and bear my witness, then, together with thousands of others, I make my influence felt for good. Says Jean Ingelow:

> I am glad to think
> I am not bound to make the world go right,
> But only to discover and to do
> With cheerful heart the work that God appoints.[2]

Dr. E. Stanley Jones says that if he had but one gift to give to the men and women of our day it would be the gift of courage, courage to live up to their convictions.

[2] Jean Ingelow, *Quotable Poems.*

(2) Again, we tend to overemphasize the value of statistics, making our denominational yearbooks into bearers of false information. But the Kingdom of God will not come through statistics, however impressive, nor will the church win battles for its Lord by means of a "paper" constituency. If we lose sight of *souls* in the rush of our ecclesiastical machinery, then God have mercy on us! The whirling of organizational wheels can never take the place of a disciplined battalion of soldiers on fire for its Lord.

An elderly lady was being shown through an imposing new church edifice. When the guide led her out again at the entrance, she asked a very pertinent question: "Have any souls been saved here lately?"

Dr. Emil Brunner points out that in proportion as the early church sought security in office, sacrament and formal creed, it lost its revolutionary power. "It ceased to be a brotherhood and became a corporation. It ceased to be a new life and became a philosophy and a theology.... It became a mere cult society in the world and ceased to work as a revolutionary ferment within the world."[3]

(3) Likewise, our Christian enterprise has lost its cutting edge because we underestimate the contribution of the layman.

Wilbur LaRoe, Jr., writes in the *Christian Century*

[3] Dr. Emil Brunner, *Eternal Hope* (Philadelphia, Westminster Press), p. 64.

(March 16, 1955) that the role of the laity was grossly underrated at the meeting of the World Council of Churches at Evanston. Everywhere one went, he says, one saw "a procession of clergymen and a multitude of priestly robes and crosses, with a handful of laymen lost in the clerical atmosphere." As one result of this professionalism in our Christian ranks, over half of the church's membership fails to attend worship on Sundays. The influence of Christian laymen is not vitally felt in secular society. And the evils of alcoholism, gambling, and juvenile delinquency flourish.

To be sure, this criticism may be exaggerated. But there is just enough truth in it to make it sting.

Seen in its true light, the church of the living God is a priesthood of believers, a vital spiritual democracy in which layman and minister serve together as brothers in Christ. In the Acts of the Apostles, Christians are quite simply described as "brethren." If laymen need to be delivered from the sin of spiritual mediocrity, ministers and church executives might well pray to be delivered from the sin of being "professionally" religious.

Those whom Jesus commanded to evangelize the world were ordinary men and women like ourselves. We do well to acknowledge that the command is still binding upon every one of us.

An elderly man heard a small boy recite Lincoln's *Gettysburg Address* with emphasis placed upon the words "of", "by" and "for", in the last sentence. "I was present when the great Commoner gave that message," he said, "and when he spoke the last sentence, he placed the emphasis on the word, 'people': 'And that government of, by and for the *people* shall not perish from the earth.' "

In this same manner, the architects of our American form of government insisted that people are the sovereign entity. The vital spiritual concept at the center of the Gospel—which nurtured our Christian-democratic tradition—is one of personal emphasis. Jesus Christ gave His life for *me*. I, therefore, live, serve and witness for *Him*. For the progress of the Kingdom of God in the world, I am responsible.

III

What are a few *frontiers* where a spiritually vital discipleship is needed?

1. There is the frontier of *Christian youth*. God has placed in our hands the salvation of our children. Think of the infinite possibilities wrapped up in their growing lives. They are our most precious asset.

I believe that young people are looking to their elders for a confident word and for the inspiration of a good example to pilot them through this era of unrest. A secret, hushed-up, clandestine discipleship will not do. Nor will large professions and little deeds.

When three young Americans who had formerly gone over to the communist side were returning home to face trial recently, it was observed that each carried a generous supply of comic books. Not a Bible, mind you, but bright-colored scraps of paper called "comic books." With these they sought to satisfy their spiritual and intellectual needs. A discerning editor pointed out at the time that it was vain for us to cry "shame" at these youngsters and to label them "turncoats" when, both ideologically and religiously, we had so ill-equipped them to live in an age of turmoil. Surely, a comic book generation is no match for this day.

We spend millions on give-away radio and television programs while we grudgingly dole out a pittance for the building of schoolrooms for our children.

Speaking of the need of clean government on the local level, the late Dr. S. Parkes Cadman once said that we expect it to be delivered at our doors with the morning's milk. We fail, somehow, to grasp that we must battle for worthwhile things.

2. There is the frontier of our *Christian world mission.* I remember seeing a picture of Hiroshima after that ill-fated city had the atomic bomb dropped upon it. It looked like some vast crater. In an area of 4.1 square miles of the city, some 78,150 persons lost their lives within a few seconds and 37,425 were injured. In the foreground of the picture, lifting its spire upwards, as if in sullen defiance, was one of the few

structures that withstood the blast: a large and beautiful church, an eloquent symbol of that "which cannot be shaken." On the tenth anniversary of the holocaust, the people of Hiroshima knelt in silent prayer around the Cenotaph, a white stone arch memorial to the dead, and prayed for peace.

When he spoke at the official opening of the sixth International Astronautical Congress at Copenhagen, the American scientist, Dr. Frederick C. Durant, remarked that the frontiers of exploration have virtually disappeared on earth. "The new frontiers," he said, "are out in another dimension."

That new dimension, let us dare to believe, is *spiritual* and lies in the unexplored regions of the human mind and heart. The destiny of humanity lies there. Christians of the world must now join hands that the Spirit of Jesus Christ may be released and make itself felt in our human relationships. We must emulate the imaginative daring of our fathers who took as their slogan, "The world for Christ in our generation."

The hour is late. Time is rapidly running out. In the words of Dr. Adolph Keller, "It is five minutes to twelve on the clock of the world's history."

Tomorrow is here!

3. There is the frontier of *church membership*, the relationship of a man to his church and—what is more—to Him who alone is Head of the great Body of Christ.

The day has arrived when we must take this sacred

relationship more seriously to heart. So much more is involved in church membership than pious gesture or social respectability.

The call of the hour is for "churchmen," in the best sense of that much abused word, for men, women, and youth who have inwardly *responded* to the call of God in Christ and who are willing to be sown as living seed in the furrows of the world's need. It is for *men* who feel their merely personal pursuits overarched by the glory of the Christian vocation, which is to bear witness to a newer and more divine order of life, the Kingdom of God. Once more, the call is for those who have ears to hear above the incessant din and clamor of the age, a Voice saying, ". . . And I, when I am lifted up from the earth, will draw all men to myself." (John 12:32).

The vital impact of Christian faith will make itself felt with new power in our world when all of us are willing to rise up and follow the great Pioneer of life into the conquests of tomorrow.

Best of all, it can happen to you, to me, to our next door neighbor. And when it does, living will have become truly and enduringly exciting!

Chapter 12

"THE BEST IS YET TO BE"—
WHY GROW OLD?

"So that thy youth is renewed like the eagle's."

(*Psalm* 103:5)

AN AMAZING address recently was delivered before the American Medical Association by an Arkansas physician, Dr. Lowry H. McDaniel. In this address, the speaker made some predictions for the year 1999, which, if valid, should completely revolutionize our thinking on the subject of age.

By the year 1999, Dr. McDaniel said, a man of ninety will be considered "young"; a man of one-hundred-and-thirty-five, "more mature," and senility, as we know it, will be at a minimum because of an improvement of the arteries. Women, thanks to proper hormone medication, will remain indefinitely young and beautiful. The much discussed and debated Salk vaccine of our day will soon be replaced by a living, modified virus vaccine. Practically all human infectious disease will be eradicated by the use of vaccines, antibiotics and multiphasic screening tests. Cancer, the most dreaded scourge of all, will be successfully treated by a virus vaccine or by radioactive compounds.

There is only one catch in all this idyllic prediction about the future by the optimistic physician from Arkansas and that lies in the area of mental health. To the solution of this problem, said he, the American Medical Association should devote itself during the last half of our century.

Now, while a lot of us welcome the hopeful predictions of medical science about men's future, we are, nevertheless, skeptical that the ultimate solution for mental illness lies in the province of the physical alone. Subtle and more intangible factors come into play in the vital area of a man's outlook on life. His operative beliefs about life in general, his faith in God, and his confidence in the future, are of crucial importance. What goes on under the surface of a man's life, in the region of the subconscious, will most importantly influence his destiny.

William James once said that the greatest revolution in his generation lay in the discovery that human beings, by changing their inner attitude of mind, can alter the outward aspect of their lives. In other words, age and youth lie not so much with our arteries as with our attitudes. In his great essay, *Is Life Worth Living*, the famous Harvard professor and philosopher concludes by saying that it all depends "on the liver."

With more and more people who are sixty-five or more in our midst than ever before, we need to take a new interest in the maturation process. One of the tragedies of our time concerns the many despondent, neglected persons huddled together like sheep in our homes for the aged. Many of them have been deserted by relatives. Some have been forgotten and are rarely visited. The light has gone from their eyes and the spring from their step. Sitting listlessly in a room reading the daily obituary column and waiting for the "grim reaper" to appear—what a tragic finale to life.

This situation need not exist. We are beginning to realize that fact and to do something about it. A new science by the name of geriatrics is coming to the fore. Conferences are being held and research is being done to determine the cause and the cure of premature senility. Actually, we never "grow" old, we allow ourselves to *drift* into old age. The old threadbare and negative terminology about age is being discarded in favor of such descriptive words as "advanced," and "elderly."

All this is to the good. Dare to believe it. Living can be indefinitely exciting—into very eternity itself.

This thrilling prospect is celebrated in the words of the 103rd psalm. The writer is making a list of his many blessings and thanking God for them. Among them is the blessing of eternal youth. He writes,

> Who forgives all your iniquity,
> Who heals all your diseases,
> Who redeems your life from the Pit,
> Who crowns you with steadfast love and mercy,
> Who satisfies you with good as long as you live,
> So that your youth is renewed like the eagle's.

> (*Psalm* 103:3–5, R.S.V.)

After reading the despairing lines of Fitzgerald's *Rubaiyat*, Robert Browning made his famous reply in the inspiring stanzas of *Rabbi Ben Ezra*. Omar sings of fate, of a "sorry scheme of things entire" which he yearns, wistfully, to "remold a little nearer the heart's desire." Browning writes of faith, faith in a God who keeps the soul eternally young by feeding it from artesian springs. What a contrast between the words of Browning and those of Fitzgerald!

> Grow old along with me!
> The best is yet to be,
> The last of life, for which the first was made.
> Our times are in his hand
> Who saith, "A whole I planned,
> Youth shows but half; trust God; see all, nor be afraid!"

None of us needs to grow "old." The best and most fruitful years can lie ahead. It is this quality of the verve

and tang and zest of life that one finds in great souls.
"It is magnificent to grow old," says Dr. Harry Emerson Fosdick, "providing one keeps young." "Never
fear old age," said the indomitable Julia Ward Howe,
"the sugar of life is at the bottom of the cup." William
Lyon Phelps, after saying that it is pathetic to see so
many persons afraid of growing old, proceeded to give
sound advice on the subject of graying hair. Were our
hair to turn green or blue, then surely we ought to see
a doctor! But when it turns gray, as nature intended,
wear it proudly like a flag. "You are fortunate," said
this great heart, "in a world of so many vicissitudes, to
have lived long enough to earn it."[1]

Consider a few suggestions which can help us keep
the spirit of eternal youth alive within ourselves.

I

We need to remember that it is the spiritual, rather
than the chronological, index in a man's life which is
most important. That is precisely what the "gerontolo-
gists" are telling us. The mind's capacity to absorb new
knowledge may be extended indefinitely. There need
be no limit when it comes to inner mind and soul

[1] Quoted in Lillian Eichler Watson, *Light from Many Lamps* (New
York, Simon and Schuster), p 270.

growth; life begins for any one of us when we make this thrilling discovery. The body may deteriorate and physical faculties abate somewhat with passing years. But the vital and essential part of us—where the real business of living goes on—the mind, can be kept alive.

This explosive discovery of the limitless capacity of the mind has destroyed many of our former ideas on education. Just to prove this fact to myself, I visited a large public library not long ago. For the most part, the chairs were filled and the tables surrounded by people in the maturer age brackets, eagerly intent on reading and study. The idea that only children can learn is rapidly becoming passé.

After referring to the outmoded idea that adult minds are too fixed and rigid to continue the learning process, Dr. Harry A. Overstreet quotes the words of Eugene Staley:

> An adult who ceases after youth to unlearn and relearn his facts, and to reconsider his opinions, is like a blindfolded person walking into a familiar room where someone has moved the furniture. Furthermore, he is a menace to a democratic society. One of the consequences of a rapidly changing world is that there is a much more important job for adult education than ever before.[2]

[2] Harry A. Overstreet, *The Mature Mind* (New York, W. W. Norton), p. 38.

Living Can Be Exciting

The greatest need of our day is for persons who are emotionally and mentally mature, who are "adult" in their reactions to the emergent situations of every day living, and who can, therefore, be entrusted with responsibility. This radiant prospect life holds out to all of us. With God's help we can all be this kind of person. You and I can have our youth renewed like the eagle's.

When you are tempted to be discouraged because of advancing years, think of what has been accomplished by the following. At seventy-four, Immanuel Kant wrote his *Anthropology, Metaphysics of Ethics*, and *Strife of the Faculties;* Tintoretto painted his *Paradise;* and Verdi produced his masterpiece, *Othello*. At eighty, Verdi produced *Falstaff*, and at eighty-five, his *Ave Maria, Stabat Mater*, and *Te Deum*. Lamarck at seventy-eight completed his great zoological work, *The Natural History of the Invertebrates*. Oliver Wendell Holmes, at seventy-nine, wrote *Over the Teacups*. Cato at eighty began the study of Greek, and Goethe completed his *Faust*. Tennyson wrote *Crossing the Bar* at eighty-three and Titian at ninety-eight painted his historic picture of the *Battle of Lepanto*.

I am not implying that we can all be shining young Apollos in our later years. We can, however, "be our age" in the best sense of that admonition. We can refuse to grow old and, instead, grow up.

II

Another way to keep mentally and spiritually young is to be an eager and enthusiastic participant in the wider sphere of life all about us.

Located, as I am, in one of the great winter resort areas of the nation, I have had a first-hand opportunity to observe some of the blighting effects of retirement. Here are John and Mary, for instance, thrilled at the prospect of being free to do as they please for the first time in their married life. Some initial contacts are made with new friends in the community of their adoption. A new home is purchased. For awhile everything seems to be going along nicely.

Soon, however, after a temporary diet of cards, tourist societies, beaching and fishing, melancholia and depression set in. Both of them feel nostalgic for the old sights and sounds. John misses the job he has left. The point is, of course, that an unplanned retirement affords too much time for brooding. What has happened to thousands of well-meaning people in this category of the disillusioned should be plain by now. God has endowed all of us with the gift of creativity. When we cease to create, we stagnate.

Nor does a second-hand participation in life, by means of radio and television, relieve the feeling of boredom. We need to sink our teeth in some form of creative activity. That is why persons by the many thousands are joining in group activities of all sorts—in religion, music, literature, athletics, etc. There are Browning clubs for those with literary inclinations; Three Quarter Century choruses for those who like to sing; "Kids and Cubs" baseball teams for those with a flare for athletics. These activities are mushrooming over the nation and elderly people are taking advantage of them. We are as old or as young as the extent of our interest in the adventure of living.

General Douglas MacArthur, not exactly a "spring chicken" himself, kept these words of Samuel Ullman placarded before him while in Tokyo:

> You are as young as your faith, as old as your doubt;
> as young as your self-confidence, as old as your fear;
> as young as your hope, as old as your despair.

Above all else, people of advanced years need to participate in purposive activities. I am fortunate in knowing many hundreds who are making their influence felt for good in the work of the church. A conference executive wrote recently asking for counsel regarding the place of elderly people in church activities. The reply I gave him may have shocked him at first: "Age is one subject we never mention around here. We are too busy living and getting things done."

Let me tell you of my friend, Louise Woodford. Instead of sitting back and taking it easy when her retirement time came, she gave herself with renewed dedication to the passion of her life, the cause of Christian world missions. Under her enthusiastic leadership, the Florida Chain of Missionary Assemblies was born. Every year she brings outstanding Christian leaders of the world to inspire us with their challenging messages. My friend has the rare gift of sparking enthusiasm in others. She has helped the rest of us to stretch our "ecumenical" muscles and to become better world citizens. Her life is tipped forwards, not backwards. For her "The best is yet to be."

III

If you would keep life zestful and creative, you must also keep alert and sensitive to the larger currents and events of your time. To live vitally and significantly in your day; to feel the winds of God in the sails of your life, however humble; to look out and see some of the great Biblical prophecies being fulfilled in the world; above all, to see history as a sphere for the operation of God's will—*that* is to have your youth renewed. It is to keep the mind alive. It is to live constantly on a new frontier.

Living Can Be Exciting

Angela Morgan in her poem *In Such an Age* celebrates this questing spirit:

> To be alive in such an age!
> With every year a lightening page
> Turned in the world's great wonder-book
> Whereon the leaning nations look
> Where men speak strong for brotherhood
> For peace and universal good;
> When miracles are everywhere
> And every inch of common air
> Throbs a tremendous prophecy
> Of greater marvels yet to be.
> O, Thrilling Age!
> O, Willing Age! [3]

The poets say so much more effectively what our pedestrian language can never convey.

While lunching in a restaurant at a great American air base, I noticed a group of airmen at a nearby table. Some of them were obviously nationals from abroad. Before them, they had spread out a map of the world. Believe me, their conversation did not languish for lack of interest or zest. Space, time and distance were no longer obstacles to those pilots. They had moved into the new world of their day and were living enthusiastically in it.

Some of us have not yet done so. Our gaze is back-

[3] Angela Morgan, "In Such an Age," *Quotable Poems* (Chicago, Willett, Clark and Colby), p. 20.

wards. Our conversation is restricted to the "good old days."

When I first entered the Christian ministry, I came to know a man whom we affectionately called "Uncle Frank." The old gentleman had been reared in the hills of Vermont and had never taken to his heart his adopted state of South Dakota. He lived only in the past and became a kind of tragic anachronism. I remember him rocking away in his little cottage, at evening time, dreamily puffing at his pipe, and saying, "When I lived in old Vermont...."

Emerson once remarked that the times are always good if we only knew what to do with them.

You and I are fortunate to have our lot cast in a time when there are strange new stirrings abroad. None other than God is shaking the foundations of things. He is asking us to "move into" our era, to help bear the burdens of humanity and, by doing so, bring His kingdom upon the earth. Those who have become a part of the "responsible society" feel springtime in their hearts. They can say with Bernard Baruch, "To me, old age is always fifteen years older than I am!"

IV

One more word: Make sure that the miracle of spiritual rebirth is constantly occurring within yourself. I believe we all need to undergo reconversion every now and then on general principles. We are as old, or as young, as our faith in God.

When Jesus said, "Blessed are the pure in heart for they shall see God," I believe that He meant that the single-eyed and the whole-visioned are the ageless. A new and dynamic conception of time has dawned on them. They are done with punching little human time clocks. They are already living the life eternal. The good news of Christ's gospel is that, however twisted and warped our lives may have become, we can be renewed by the Holy Spirit.

The best years of our lives can lie ahead. What if the snows of winter be on our heads so long as eternal youth be in our hearts?

You should meet my friend, Frank Boyd, famous posture expert and author of *The Fine Art of Living*. At eighty-eight he has retained the alacrity of a boy of fifteen. He is hard at work, every day of his life, helping men and women renew their youth. He plans, before long, to write another book. His gaze is toward the future.

When Frank Lloyd Wright, the well-known architect, was asked what he would select as his masterpiece, he replied, "My next one." Living is truly exciting for people of this kind.

To realize that our spiritual age, rather than our chronological, is what counts most; to share vitally and unselfishly in the larger life all around us; to be alert to the stirrings of a new world in the making; to feel God's Spirit at work within ourselves—*that* is to retain the spirit of eternal youth.

Then, why grow old? Say instead with Henry Van Dyke:

> So let the way wind up the hill or down,
> O'er rough or smooth, the journey will be joy;
> Still seeking what I sought when but a boy,
> New friendship, high adventure, and a crown,
> I shall grow old, but never lose life's zest,
> Because the road's last turn will be the best!

Chapter 13

THE WAY OUT OF OUR WORRIES

"So don't worry—Set your heart on His Kingdom
and His goodness, and all these things will come
to you as a matter of course."

(Matt. 6:31, 33,
J. B. Phillips's Translation)

A CHAPLAIN had a sign posted on his door: "If you have
worries, come in and let's talk them over. If not, come
in and tell us how you do it!"

Dr. E. Stanley Jones tells of a woman who had
become such a confirmed worrier that her very brain
cells began to atrophy and decay under the strain. The
life forces started to break down because of her
"retreatism," her abject fear of life. The doctors finally
decided to remove that part of her brain which presides
over foresight. When it was suggested that she might
be healed through the regenerating power of religious

faith, and escape surgery, she vigorously objected, saying that such a course might have been possible ten years ago but that it was too late now.[1]

Of course, she was wrong, dead wrong. It is never "too late" to begin the life of trust; never too late to step out of the structure of fear and anxiety into the life of faith. In fact, Jesus' words, "Don't worry" are a command. God wills for us a life unencumbered by false cares. Actually, worry is disobedience. It is living, to all intents, as though God were not. It is unbelief.

Perhaps I may be permitted a personal admission at this point. Not until I had been in the Christian ministry for some years did Jesus' teaching about the futility of worry really dawn on me. Oh yes, I had been reared on the Sermon on the Mount and had willingly acknowledged its poetic beauty and vivid imagery. I did everything with the Sermon on the Mount but accept it as an actual way of living. And so, like some who may read these words, I would close my Bible after reading its message and go right back into my pedestrian life of pushing and fretting and doubting.

How many there are—some of them members of a Christian church—who admire the teaching of Jesus as a lovely ideal but who have yet to accept it as an actual way of living!

Then one day, light began to break in on my confused mind. I saw that the way *out* of worry is the way

1 E. Stanley Jones, *Abundant Living*, p. 101.

up into believing trust. I had had too much on my mind and not enough in my heart. The overall cure for worry is contained in the words of Jesus about the Kingdom of God. How I could have been oblivious to their meaning for so long a time I cannot explain, unless it be our common human frailty that seeks to dodge the truth rather than face it. Like "peace of mind," the "worry-less" life could be had—on God's terms.

I had insisted on living life my own way, rather than Christ's way, on seeking first my petty little kingdom of self rather than the transcendent Kingdom of which Christ is sovereign. Jesus' words struck inward on my mind like hammer blows: "So don't worry—set your heart, your affections, on God's Kingdom and God's goodness and whatever else you may need will come to you as a matter of course."

Dr. George A. Buttrick says, "There is a Franciscan element in all true Christianity. Most of us who call ourselves Christians fail sadly in this joyous trust in God."[2]

True indeed. But once put your feet on this new and living way of faith and trust taught by Jesus and you find yourself led out of darkness into the light. If you stumble, as we all must at times, you can get to your feet again and, with heaven's help, continue toward the light. In the Christian life, as elsewhere, not

[2] George A. Buttrick, *Interpreter's Bible*, Vol. 7, pp. 323-4.

"failure but low aim is crime." God mercifully judges by the inner intent of our hearts.

I

Let us begin our study of the life of trust by stating the argument in reverse.

When our Lord commands us not to worry, He is not putting a premium on *shiftlessness*. The life of faith is not a life of indolence, of allowing someone else to carry our share of life's load. We are not to be Micawbers, idly waiting for something to turn up. The One who commands us not to be anxious was Himself journeying toward a cross. He knew, as none other has ever known, the full meaning of responsibility.

Nor is the carefree life one of callous *indifference* toward the welfare of others who may be in need of our help. The Christian does not walk through life with hoodwinked eyes and stopped-up ears. Margaret Slattery, friend and counselor of youth, once wrote of the Master that "He took it upon himself." That is, He voluntarily assumed the burden of the world's woes and sufferings and sins. In Him,

> Desperate tides of the world's great anguish
> Were forced through the channel of a single heart.

The Christian life, when faithfully lived, can never be one of neutralism or indifference.

Once more, Christian living is not *fatalism*. There is a kind of religious Stoicism that walks its melancholy way with head "bloody but unbowed." It holds that the best response to life is one of utter resignation. A man remarked of a friend of his who had been killed in a car accident that "his number was up, his time had come." No reference was made to the element of human sin and folly involved in the mishap. Those who hold to this attitude of fatalism—and they are more numerous than we dare to think—deny the fatherly providence of God and dub themselves soulless marionettes. They only darken the way of counsel.

II

Stated in positive terms, then, what is Jesus' teaching about the life of trust?

(1) First, his teaching concerns *priorities*. We are to let God put the really great things at the center of our lives—His Kingdom and His Goodness—and trust Him to supply the lesser needs as a matter of course. In the literature of the early church there appeared this unwritten saying of Jesus: "Ask the great things and the

little will be added unto you; ask the heavenly things and the earthly will be added unto you."[3]

The unworried life cannot be found by seeking it directly. It follows as a result of an act of complete commitment on our part. "Seek first His Kingdom." Settle that first.

Often it is overconcern about *marginal* matters that puts wrinkles on our foreheads and weights on our hearts. It is our worldly-mindedness, according to Jesus, that lands us in the quagmire of anxiety. "For after all these things do the pagans seek, and furthermore, your heavenly Father knows your needs." (Matt. 6:32).

We are concerned about our health and the well-being of our loved ones; about financial matters; about our reputations and what others say and think about us; about success in our appointed tasks—to mention only a few things. And right there, Jesus insists, lies the *root* of our trouble .These things are not of supreme importance. Something infinitely greater must occupy the center of our lives. We are to get the Kingdom pattern into our daily thinking and living, to set our hearts on Christ and the Kingdom of God. Then only shall we get our lives into spiritual focus and see things in true perspective. Then we shall stop making "mountains out of molehills" and "molehills out of moun-

[3] David Smith, *Commentary on Matthew* (New York, Doubleday Doran, 1928), p. 125.

tains." Then we shall see life "steadily and see it whole."

For some of us this may mean a radical revision of our values, a complete and utter reorientation of our lives Godward. Only when that happens to us can we see on what a self-centered plane we have been living. And a new sense of inner release and freedom will thrill us through.

But, one asks, does this way of life really work out in a "dog eat dog, devil take the hindmost" kind of human society? One can imagine a smile on the Master's face as he quietly answers, "But, my child, you have tried the other ways only to find them futile. What shall it profit you if you gain the world and lose your soul? What will you give in exchange for your soul?"

Many of our leading physicians and surgeons today would agree that only the Christian way really works.

The stomach ulcer has been called the wound stripe of our civilization. A noted commentator says that many of us, especially in our crowded cities, are oppressed with "civilization sickness." A young business executive, facing a severe heart operation because of complete exhaustion, was overheard to exclaim, "But I made it!" He had, it is true, battled his way to a higher salary bracket—but at what cost! Not that business and the honest accumulation of money are evil in themselves. We get into trouble at the point where we worship them as gods.

The Way Out Of Our Worries

On the occasion of his eightieth birthday, Mr. J. C. Penney offered some wise counsel to young men and women about to enter the business world. He urged them to put real living first, to put God and the Kingdom at the center of their lives, and not to be taken in by the largest salary offer.

(2) Our second bit of counsel is contained in the well-known but little obeyed words of Jesus: "Don't worry at all, then, about *tomorrow*. One day's trouble is enough for the day—and tomorrow will look after itself."

Positively stated, this is a command to *live a day at a time*, with a humble, childlike trust in the fatherly providence of the Almighty. The proud and the self-opinionated will refuse to accept this teaching: the humble will receive it with eagerness. Don't telescope your responsibilities into an hour or a day. Jesus is saying, walk life's way with joyous abandon, a step at a time, with your trust in God.

When he addressed the members of the United States Supreme Court recently, Dr. Ralph W. Sockman told the story of a little boy who was walking through heavy downtown traffic with his father. Looking with fondness into his father's face, he said, "I'm just a little boy and my hand might let go; but you, my father, are big and strong, and your hand won't let go."

George Klingle imparts the same wise counsel for Christian living in his poem *Hour by Hour*.

God broke our years to hours and days, that
      Hour by hour
      And day by day,
We might be able all along
To keep quite strong.
Should all the weight of life
Be laid across our shoulders, and the future, rife
With woe and struggle, meet us face to face
      At just one place,
      We could not go;
Our feet would stop; and so
God lays a little on us every day.
And never, I believe, on all the way,
Will burdens bear so deep
Or pathways lie so steep
But we can go, if by God's power,
We only bear the burden by the hour.[4]

Those who have learned to trust in God's loving providence know why Jesus made mention of the gaiety of birds, the beauty of flowers, and the shining faces of little children in his teaching about the carefree life. Instead of fretting about life, they live it, celebrate it, play it out like music! The flowers and the birds and the children know themselves to be an organic part of

[4] George Klingle, "Hour by Hour," *Quotable Poems* (Chicago, Willett, Clark and Colby), Vol. 1, p. 71.

the great symphony of creation which lives by praising and adoring the Creator. God cares for them. "Alas, you of little faith, you do not seem to grasp that you are infinitely more precious to God than sparrows and flowers."

Bishop Gerald Kennedy says that a new day dawned for him when he found that he could rest all his cares and anxieties back on the omnipotent heart of God and live by faith, a day at a time.

A friend once told me the secret of her radiant and effective life. Every morning she takes her task fresh from the hands of God in the spirit of prayer. At evening time she lays it down again with thanksgiving, at the Master's feet. Thus she walks the high road of faith.

(3) This way of living also makes of the future an exciting adventure with God. We no longer look forward with fear at what the future may hold in store, for our lives are "hid with Christ in God." Such day by day living has the feel of the eternal in it. Nor do we need to push or fret, for God unfolds the way. He is in the tomorrows; therefore, we journey toward them in joyous expectancy. Enough for us to say with Tennyson:

> I know not where his islands lift their fronded palms in air,
> I only know I cannot drift beyond his love and care.

At one stage in his career, J. C. Penney, mentioned before, felt himself a complete failure. The bottom had fallen out of his financial securities, and the huge empire of business he had erected appeared headed for collapse. Like many another "successful" business man, he came to the poignant realization that he had left out something of vital and primary importance along the way, that lasting security must share the nature of the spiritual.

While a patient at the Battle Creek Sanitarium, he actually felt one night that the end might not be far away. With what seemed his remaining strength, he wrote a last message to his family.

Then, at this breaking point, his extremity became God's opportunity. Early the next morning he heard voices in a distant part of the building singing a beloved hymn:

> No matter what may be the test,
> God will take care of you.
> Lean, weary one, upon his breast,
> God will take care of you.

Something happened to J. C. Penney in the little prayer chapel that morning that he can never explain. He prefers to call it a miracle. He had come to the end of his futile, human way. Now, God, with His boundless love and mercy was pointing to a new and thrilling future.

A weight lifted from my spirit. I came out of that room a different man, renewed. I had gone in bowed with a paralysis of spirit, utterly adrift. I came forth with a soaring sense of release, from a bondage of gathering death to a pulse of hopeful living. I had glimpsed God.[5]

Some who read these words of testimony may have already had their "Battle Creek" experience, their Damascus Road awakening. Others may still need to undergo it.

What is involved in such an experience is a rightful ordering of our lives with regard to the priorities, the really great and lasting things.

Once our hearts are *set* on God's Kingdom and Goodness, on Christ's rulership for our lives, burdens that had oppressed us are lifted. New stamina and strength well into our hearts. We take up our tasks with a new fortitude. Nothing can any longer defeat us.

The way out of worry has become the way *up* into faith.

[5] J. C. Penney, *Fifty Years with the Golden Rule* (New York, Harper & Brothers, 1950), p. 159.

177

Chapter 14

THE REAL MEANING OF HAPPINESS

"Rejoice that your names are written in heaven!"

(Luke 10:20)

A MAN who was visiting a friend at the latter's luxurious summer place came upon his host one evening looking with wistful eyes upon hills in the distance. The Supreme Artist had flung the mantle of His beauty over the scene: birds gaily singing their vespers; huge bouquets of flowers in the garden plots surrounding the house; and the rare pageantry of a sunset about to take place. "You must be very happy in this beautiful place," remarked the guest. There was a moment of silence, and then the reply: "Happy? Is anyone ever really happy?"

I can remember the halcyon days of college when we students would hold prolonged discussions on the subject of happiness. We would quote Epictetus, the Greek

178

slave, who wrote among his famous sayings that if a man is unhappy, his unhappiness is his own fault, for God made all men to be happy. And then, of course, there was that wise saying of Abraham Lincoln that a man is about as happy as he makes up his mind to be.

Many in this bewildering day in which we live are frankly doubting even the possibility of happiness. Suicide rates are alarmingly high, an evident token of the frustration in many lives. "Most men," wrote Henry David Thoreau, "live their lives out in quiet desperation." As a matter of fact, how can anyone be expected to be happy in such a sorry, makeshift world? The modern mood, whatever else may be said of it, is hardly one of jubilation.

Read the New Testament and you will not find the word "happiness" used as such. The most radiantly happy Man who ever lived employed, instead, such descriptive terms as "life," "treasure," "joy": words with a deeper connotation of meaning. The sheer glory of living which so overflowed the hearts of Jesus' followers would hardly come within the context of much that we call happiness in our day. In fact, even some of the disciples of Jesus got off on the wrong foot when it came to happiness. Call to mind the seventy Jesus sent out on the first great preaching mission of Christian history. When they returned, their hearts were filled with a false sense of pride. Just listen to them: "Lord, even the demons are subject unto us in your name!" These men had seen a revelation of *power* that would put the atomic bomb to shame. They had tasted the powers of the age to come. God had wrought miracles of healing and deliverance through them. But what they had witnessed, instead of humbling them, had blinded their eyes and dulled their hearts to the real meaning of joy and power.

One can imagine Jesus listening to them patiently. He had indeed conferred on them the power to heal; had trusted them with it in order that God might be glorified and the enslaved set free. It was the cancer of false pride—that futile boasting—that grieved His heart. He said to them:

> I saw Satan fall like lightning from heaven. Behold I have given you authority to tread upon serpents and scorpions, and over all the power of the enemy; and nothing shall hurt you. Nevertheless, do not rejoice in this, that the spirits are subject to you; but rejoice that your names are written in heaven.　　(Luke 10:17–20).

To be obsessed with power and position as ends in themselves is not to know happiness. It was pride that made Satan fall "like lightning from heaven." These, his disciples, were to rejoice not because of their God-given power over evil spirits but because their names were "written in heaven."

In these words, the Master gives us the one perfect recipe for happiness. To be reckoned among the children of God through sheer grace! To have tasted, if only a little, the precious gift of salvation! To be filled with a Christ-like concern and compassion for the sick, sorrowing, and suffering is to know true rejoicing. It is to have your name inscribed among the fortunate ones of the earth.

That leaves a lot of us on the outer fringe of happiness, doesn't it? We fail to search where the true and lasting joys are to be found. The words of a once-popular ditty quite aptly portray the modern mood of disenchantment, "I'm forever chasing rainbows."

The renowned clown, Grimaldi, was privately one of the most miserable men who ever lived. Like many of us, he had a hard time getting along with himself. He finally sought a counselor, asking for some rare talisman that might dispel his inward wretchedness. He was told to go and listen to a famous clown by the name of Grimaldi and he would laugh away his troubles in sheer delight! "Alas," said the luckless clown, "I am that wretched man."

In our incessant clamoring after happiness we would do well to remember that incident. The very ardor of our pursuit of happiness may be the reason that it so often eludes our grasp. Josh Billings used to say that if we ever find happiness by hunting for it, we will find it, as the old woman did her lost spectacles, safe on her nose all the time.

The Christian martyrs scrawled one word above all

others on the walls of the Roman catacombs where they had been driven. The word was "Vita," (Life.) The joy that was in Christ had entered into them. They were an hilarious people—the word stems from the Greek word *hilaros*, meaning joyful. The good news of God had come their way. Not even the horrors of persecution or the arena could dispel their joy.

Have we moderns, then, lost the capacity to experience their joy? Have we lost sight of those invisibles and intangibles which alone can rid our lives of pedestrianism? To ask these questions is almost to answer them. At any rate, let us dare bring ourselves to Jesus and we shall find out that our names, too, may be "written in heaven."

I

If you would know real happiness, you must make it a practice to be thankful for the simple, recurring blessings of every day—never take them for granted. One recalls the words of George Lorimer, that it is nice to have sufficient money for the necessities of life but that we need to pause, occasionally, and thank God for the things that money cannot buy.

We, here, in richly blessed America, especially need a new philosophy of happiness. Stop for a moment and think: the richest blessings in your life can never be purchased across a counter—the love of dear ones in the home, the beauty of earth and sky, the loyalty of friends who have proven themselves, the peace of God which passes all understanding. These constitute the inner soul-wealth that makes life really worthwhile.

Sitting at the door of his little shack at Walden, Henry David Thoreau, that tireless advocate of the simple life, could say, "I love best to have each thing in its season, doing without it at all other times. I have never got over my surprise that I should have been born into the most estimable place in all the world, and in the nick of time too." More than anything else, we need to simplify our wants and look out again upon life in all its richness with appreciative eyes and grateful hearts. "Earth's crammed with heaven, and every common bush [is] aflame with God," did we only realize it.

When all is said and done, the happy people are those who know with Jesus that contentment does not spring from the multiplication of gadgets, however clever, but from the cultivation of those inner, spiritual values that defy time and tide.

A little aged saint of my acquaintance lives in an out-of-the-way woodshed. A visit in her home—for she has made it that—is a rare treat. The many books and magazines sprawled about are evidence of her broad interest in life. Her little radio keeps her in touch with world events. She is a faithful member and regular attendant of her church. She even manages to give generously out of her scant savings for the various enterprises of her church.

The secret of her rare spirit of happiness is to be found in the fact that she had reduced her wants to essential needs. Her many troven treasures are within herself. She is a convincing example of one who lives the uncluttered life. At the center of her life and heart lies deep contentment. She demonstrates in a practical way what Stevenson called the "great theorem of the livableness of life."

By way of contrast, Howard Whitman tells of the wealthy businessman whose wife was always clamoring for more things. Being a man of great foresight, he purchased a family lot in the local cemetery and even asked that suitable epitaphs be inscribed on the grave markers. When asked what words should be put on his wife's tombstone, he said, "Write—'She died of things.'" Asked for his own epitaph, he said, "Just write, 'He died providing them!'"

In Maeterlinck's play, *The Blue Bird*, Tyltyl and Mytyl, the woodcutter's children, search far and wide for happiness only to return and find it on their own doorstep. Many a disappointed person in our day would do well to repeat the words of the woodcutter's children: "We went so far and it [happiness] was here all the time."

II

The happy people are also those who, as W. Beran Wolfe used to say, find their happiness in a focus *outside* of themselves.

Dr. Wolfe, distinguished young psychiatrist, spoke out of experience of long and intimate dealing with the troubles of people. "I'm lonely." "I hate my job." "I have no time for friends." "I feel like committing suicide." These are but a few of the despairing complaints his patients brought to him. And the gist of the counsel he found himself giving his patients may be simply stated thus: "To find happiness we must seek for it in a focus outside ourselves." Think for a moment of some of the buoyant, enthusiastic and radiant persons you know. They are the ones who have learned the art, perhaps through much inner travail and trouble, of living outside of themselves. They are quite literally "self-forgot in serving other's needs."

Whenever Helen Keller lectures, as she often does, on the subject of happiness, an opportunity is given her listeners to ask questions. On one such occasion, a man asked, "Miss Keller, can you feel colors?" "Yes," came the reply. "I can feel blue."

Like the rest of us, Helen Keller could feel sorry for herself. Many a lesser soul would do so in her circumstances. But, great soul that she is, she has learned to live in a focus outside of herself. She is far too busy sharing the secret of her radiant life with others to gaze morbidly inward on herself. "Happiness," said Emerson, "is a perfume you cannot pour on others without getting a few drops on yourself."

Blessed beyond all words are those who, like Helen Keller, have learned to get themselves off their own hands by giving themselves away. They are fulfilling the deepest law of their own being. Their names are "written in heaven."

This is not to say, however, that we should ever engage in some form of social service in order that the slack might be taken out of our lives. Bored people never make radiant Christian witnesses. There is a kind of philanthropy abroad in the world today that has the dull metallic clank of the cash register in it. It was of that kind of giving that Jesus said, "Verily, they have their reward." The heart is not in it.

Dr. Leslie Weatherhead once told of a London slum mother who was visited by a woman who had rather suddenly taken up with religion. Exasperated beyond words by the repeated visits of this officious woman, the slum mother wrote to the parish vicar saying, "Please tell Mrs. So and So to stop saving her soul on me."

Whenever our service to others, be it even in the church, becomes cold, impersonal, and dutiful, it is no longer Christian. In Dwight L. Moody's fine phrase,

"We must let love be the motive power in all that we do for God." And love—the spirit of Agape, as the first Christians knew it—is warm, personal and concrete in its bestowals. It gets us outside ourselves and into the lives of others. We know that we have passed "out of death into life because we love the brethren." (I John 3:14). Such was—and is—the apostolic joy. It is something that spills over.

A small boy living in a London attic was telling a social worker about a kindly man who sometimes came to see him. "He even reads the Bible to me and prays with me." When asked if he knew the man's name, he hesitated a bit and then added, "I'm not sure, but if I remember correctly, he said his name was Gladstone." The famous statesman found time in his busy schedule to take a personal interest in a London slum child.

Once put your arm around another in need of the Christian love and sympathy you can give and you will know happiness. The words of Elizabeth Barrett Browning will describe your new found joy:

> A child's kiss
> Set on thy sighing lips shall make thee glad;
> A poor man served by thee shall make thee rich;
> A sick man helped by thee shall make thee strong;
> Thou shalt be served thyself by every sense
> Of service which thou renderest.

Yes, and nearby stands the Master, a smile upon His face, saying, "Inasmuch as you did it unto the least of these my brethren, you did it unto me." (Matt. 25:40). We have become outgoing in spirit and so we have found joy.

III

There may be some of us, however, for whom the ordinary channels of service are no longer open. Our lot may even be cast on an invalid's couch or chair, or we may have arrived at an age when participation in the work of our church or community must be limited.

What, then? Suppose we let the answer to that question be stated in a memorable phrase of Thomas Carlyle: "There is in man a *higher* than love of happiness; he can do without happiness, and instead, thereof, find blessedness."

"Blessedness?" But what, we ask, is the actual meaning of that much used word? Isn't it a term used only by religious professionals, the stock in trade of mystics? What can it possibly have to do with life?

The answer is, everything. When Jesus spoke in his Sermon on the Mount of the meek, the poor in spirit, the pure in heart and the persecuted as being "blessed," he was talking about ordinary people like ourselves.

The Real Meaning Of Happiness

The blessed ones are the happy ones because the joy of Christ has entered as a living reality into their lives. They have learned to love God for Himself. They know of the spiritual power that can be released through prayer and so they do not feel useless. Once this miracle of faith and new birth takes place in our lives, we gladly forgo the tawdry, shallow pleasures of the world. We have cast our lot with the "joys that through all times abide." There is a searching and profound meaning in the words of the Shorter Catechism for those who will learn it: "The chief end of man is to glorify God and to enjoy him forever."

Dr. John Henry Jowett used to tell of a man who for many years had faithfully served his church as a deacon. In time, a severe illness made it impossible for him to attend his church any longer. His pastor would occasionally drop in for a visit. When the ill man could no longer engage in conversation because of a throat ailment, he asked for a sheet of paper, wrote some words upon it, and handed it to his pastor. He had written the words of the psalmist, "Oh that men would praise the Lord for his goodness and for his wonderful works to the children of men." He had found blessedness, the joy that neither illness nor death can despoil.

How, then, do we find real happiness? By recognizing the simple joys of life when they come our way and by being grateful for them. By finding a focus for our happiness outside of ourselves in the love and service of others. But, most of all, by tasting that rarest form of happiness called blessedness, the very life of God in our souls.

That joy is open to all of us. Our names may be "written in heaven."

Chapter 15

PRAYER, THE SOLUTION
TO ALL OUR PROBLEMS

"Ask, and you will receive, that your joy may be full."

(*John* 16:24)

SOME who read these words will remember a book entitled *The Raft*. It contains an account of three men adrift in a rubber boat hundreds of miles out on the Pacific. These men were U. S. Navy fliers whose plane had sunk so fast that the occupants hardly had had time to launch their lifeboat. After being adrift for many days and nights, one of their number suggested that they pray. They were ordinary men, like ourselves, raised for the most part in Christian homes but who had strayed from their childhood faith. The suggestion of prayer proved so helpful that they decided on a prayer time every day. "There was comfort," said the leader, "in passing our burden to Someone bigger than ourselves in this empty vastness."[1]

These words describe the way many of us feel in these demanding days. There is the "empty vastness" of our many personal problems, of our divided and disgruntled world, of our home, business and professional lives.

A little girl after listening to her parents discuss their many troubles was overheard to offer the following bedtime prayer: "And now, Dear Lord, be sure and look after yourself, for if anything happens to you, we're all sunk!"

The average man you meet has at least a faint belief in prayer, a kind of irreducible minimum which sees him over the hard stretches. Once he knelt at his mother's knee and said his "Now I lay me." But the years with their accumulated disappointments have rather sadly dented and dimmed that belief. He has failed, somehow, to throw the right "switches." Like many of us, he listens wistfully when others describe the rich blessings prayer has brought into their lives. If only their experience might become his!

Still others are unduly concerned with theoretical questions *about* prayer, making a problem out of what was meant to be a beneficence. There is the question of the aesthetics of prayer and there is that old bugaboo of the relationship of science and religion. How often

[1] Robert Trumbull, *The Raft* (New York, Henry Holt, 1942).

we resemble a party of bathers on holiday near a delectable ocean, arguing about the chemical properties of water. Or, to change the figure somewhat, we are like men lost in a jungle who need to push up through the underbrush of supposition and theory into the clear light of experience and realization. Hungry men need to have food set before them and thirsty men require water. Oh, to "stoop down, and drink, and live!"[1]

In all our bafflement, we do well to remember that Jesus never argued about prayer: He prayed. He likewise commanded His disciples to pray in confidence to a heavenly Father who would respond to their entreaties. "Ask," said He, "and you will receive, that your joy may be full." We are to bring our little buckets of human need and dip them into the ocean of heaven's abundance. We may bring our burdened little lives and refresh them at the Wellspring of life. "Ask—Receive!" It is a command issuing in healing and salvation.

Unaided and alone, we are no match for life. But opened and surrendered to God through the medium of prayer, He can work miracles through us. We learn the "ability which God gives." (I Peter 4:11).

That is why thousands are turning with renewed interest to prayer in our time. Where else shall we go with our heavy burdens? Christ has the words of eternal life—and He alone.

[1] From the hymn, *I Heard the Voice of Jesus Say*, by John B. Dykes.

Through a living communion with God these questing thousands are finding deliverance from trials, worries, and cares. With James Russell Lowell they are discovering a "mystery of purpose gleaming through the secular confusions of the world." [2]

A patient in a large city hospital told, with shining eyes, how his surgeon had prayed at his bedside the night before the operation was to take place.

"As a physician," wrote Dr. Alexis Carrel, "I have seen men, after every other therapy has failed, lifted out of disease and melancholy by the serene effort of prayer." The renowned physician-scientist went on to assert that we link ourselves through prayer with the power that spins the universe.

Dr. Glenn Clark, great spiritual leader, urges us to pray the prayer of faith and then, like the parachutist, to jump right off into the surrounding atmosphere confident that we shall be sustained. It is that vital sense of *venture* in prayer that we need to gain. Von Hugel used to say that real religion begins with a man alone on his knees in the presence of God. The great souls of the race have always held that spiritual power alone is supreme, and that man, the child of God, can avail himself of that power through prayer.

However weak and inadequate our lives may seem to be, they can be completely revolutionized and

[2] James Russell Lowell, "Intimations," *Poems for Life* (Chicago, Willett, Clark and Colby), p. 64.

revitalized through the grace of prayer. None other than Jesus himself, greatest of all pray-ers, gives us this assurance.

Truly, truly, I say to you, if you ask anything of the Father, he will give it to you in my name. Hitherto, you have asked nothing in my name; ask, and you will receive, that your joy may be full.[3]

In this chapter let us dare to stake out some claims in this most essential area of the Christian life.

I

The "kneeling people," as someone has called them, have found a clue to the meaning and mystery of existence in this world. Once our lives are opened heavenward through prayer, we find assuagement for the "home sickness" that is within us. Like Robinson Crusoe, stranded and alone on his island, we discover a "footprint" on the sands of time and know that we are not alone as we face the perils of life's pilgrimage. We have found a light to guide us on our way.

It does not matter that *your* method and manner of praying differ from *mine*. A great preacher of our generation was invited by a friend to share his prayer-time. Instead of kneeling in the orthodox manner, this

[3] John 16:23, 24.

man sat at his piano, and as he played, he prayed. Henry Ward Beecher used to say of his organist at Plymouth Church that when his fingers swept the console, men found themselves in the presence of God. He prayed with his fingers.

Jesus bids us come and knock at heaven's gate, each in the way best suited to him. And once the door is opened from within, we experience the reality and the wonder of prayer. Burdens are lifted. Horizons are broadened. Prayer ceases to be a theory and becomes a friendship, a vital, first-hand encounter with reality, a very breath blown to us from the heights. "Prayer," said Dwight L. Moody, "is just opening the door of your heart and letting Christ come in." God himself fills the "empty vastness" of our lives, and with Whittier we discover:

> . . . an eternal Good which overlies
> The sorrow of the world, Love which outlives
> All sin and wrong, Compassion which forgives
> To the uttermost, and Justice whose clear eyes
> Through lapse and failure look to the intent,
> And judge our failure by the life we meant.[4]

When the wife of a nationally known college president recently visited our church, I could not help noticing the outgoing quality of her life and her radiant and contagious spirit.

For many years she had been a nominal Christian,

[4] J. G. Whittier, "At Eventide," *Poems for Life, op. cit.,* p. 175.

just "good enough to get by." She belonged to the category of those who have enough religion to make them miserable. Her name appeared on a church membership roll. She had served on many a committee. One day it was her good fortune to meet a missionary and his wife, both radiant Christians, who had just returned from service abroad. Sensing her need, they led her into a kindling, personal experience of God's love in Christ. She learned to pray the prayer of faith. The actual presence and power of Jesus Christ entered her life to stay. Now she is busy leading others into the joy of her own discovery. The light shone in her eyes as she offered her testimony. She had found a clue to life's inner meaning and purpose. She was no longer alone.

II

Prayer, as Jesus taught it, is also the solution for the misunderstandings that arise between us.

The atmosphere of our day is beset with friction, suspicion, and hatred. We get on each other's nerves and in each other's way. You can fairly feel animosity as you drive through heavy traffic on your way to work every morning.

Now, prayer is a special grace in that it affords us a reprieve from this foul and vicious circle of hatred and recrimination. It breaks right through that circle with the redeeming love and forgiveness of God. At the foot of Christ's Cross, we find pardon both for ourselves and those who have wronged us. We learn again the meaning of the words, "forgiving one another, even as God for Christ's sake has forgiven you." (Eph. 4:32).

You simply cannot cherish a spirit of ill will against another person once you have held him before God in prayer, in obedience to Jesus' command that you pray for those who have despitefully used you. The fact is, you can hardly wait to get to your brother that you may forgive him and, in turn, receive his forgiveness.

It was said of a certain saint that prayer had become so fixed a habit in his life that his very thoughts of others turned to prayers.

A woman came to our counseling room to say that she felt her life a dismal failure. The reason soon became apparent. She had been badly hurt in her human relationships. "I hate human beings," she said, "they get on my nerves so." After a time of counseling, we knelt together before a cross in the little prayer chapel of the church, asking God to take away the heart of stone and replace it with a heart of love and compassion. Before long, she was able to rise up and say that she felt a heavy burden had been lifted from her heart, that she felt a quickening of the spirit of love in her inner being. She could love others now in the love of God. Praying hearts, remember, are forgiving hearts.

An instance of how prayer can redeem lives from pettiness was given by Dr. E. Stanley Jones. A disgruntled couple stalked into a music store intent on renting a player piano. They had laid up a bountiful supply of liquor and would have one more fling before separating. The salesman who waited upon them sensed the nature of their difficulty. Soon they were telling him their troubles, spilling it out like a torrent. In the rear of the store they knelt and quietly gave themselves anew to God and to each other. Honest self-searching prayer became the means of redeeming a marriage and salvaging a home. God's love had entered into a situation no human agency could heal and had transformed it.

A friend who serves as a consultant in marriage relations says that once he can get his counselees to look at life from a center *outside* of themselves, reconciliation is close at hand. Prayer makes it possible for us to do this. For "with God nothing is impossible."

III

People are also discovering, in the great renaissance of prayer that is taking place, that habitual communion with God takes the strain out of living. Burdens that had seemed too heavy to bear became strangely light. The very act of prayer ushers the suppliant into a realm of life in which mercy, strength and power are infinitely available.

Walter Rauschenbusch, prophet of social righteousness, was one of the most misunderstood and maligned men of his generation. Yet, in spite of persecution and ill health, he found staying power through the daily, hourly habit he had formed of inwardly communing with God. The secret of his life is fortunately preserved for us in a poem from his pen, entitled *The Little Gate To God*.

> In the great quiet of God,
> My troubles are but pebbles on the road,
> My joys are like the everlasting hills.
> So it is when I step through the gate of prayer,
> From time into eternity.[5]

Rauschenbusch knew the ground swell of the Spirit in his soul. He prevailed, as great souls always have, through prayer.

Kagawa, great burden-bearer of the Japanese people, rises each morning at four o'clock for an hour of quiet meditation. He drinks deeply at the wellspring of God's power. Then this seemingly frail little man proceeds to walk through the day with a fearless and serene heart.

Prayer brings to our lives the thrust of spiritual sinews. It aligns our lives with a strength not our own.

[5] Walter Rauschenbusch, "The Little Gate To God," *Poems for Life. Ibid.*, p. 168.

When life gets too hard for us and we are about to give up, we should recall the prayer of a humble Negro preacher: "Lord, there isn't anything can be too hard for You and me—together."

IV

This chapter began with an account of three men adrift on a raft. Today it would seem that all of humanity is lost and adrift on a "raft." An earnest Christian woman who had listened to an address on the menace of communism said to her pastor, "Everything looks so hopeless, doesn't it?"

But man's extremity has always been God's opportunity. The historian tells us that the Protestant Reformation began in the prayer closet of Martin Luther. Look out on the world through eyes which prayer has opened and new vistas of hope beckon. Prayer offered from a contrite heart, however burdened, puts a new face on things. The "kneeling people" actually bring new events to pass. New emergents of hope spring up as, in obedience to their Lord's command, they pray for the kingdom to come.

Paul, when he prayed, beheld the whole creation undergoing a cosmic travail. A new race was appearing and a new world was being born. Notice that word "new!" It is an indispensable term in our Christian vocabulary of hope. Someone has said that the early Christians went out from their knees "hurling their lives after their prayers."

Professor Arnold Toynbee tells us that the law of the universe for our human race may be stated thus: Rise to a higher level, or perish. The ultimate meaning of history, he says, is couched in these words. So long as we fight communism with its own materialistic weapons we shall get nowhere. Prosperity, as we like to think of it in the West, and physical arsenals, are not enough.

> All valiant dust that builds on dust,
> And guarding calls not thee to guard.

But the grace of God—says the famous historian—could work the needed miracle. And that miracle, it must be added, can be released only through prayer.

When he spoke before the World Council of Churches at Evanston in 1954, President Eisenhower gave eloquent testimony to his deep faith in the power of prayer. "Our goal," said he, "should be nothing short of inviting every single person in every single country, who believes in a Supreme Being, to join in this mighty intense act of faith." The President continued, "If this mass dedication launched an unending campaign for peace, supported by prayer, I am certain wondrous results would ensue."

The words of the American President bring the "new

crusade" to our every doorstep. A revival of earnest prayer could bring order out of the world's chaos.

A chaplain who had been the effective means of leading thousands of communist prisoners into the Christian fold was asked how he did it. His reply was revealing: "I did not try to sweep out the darkness; I just let in the light."

When God gave us the gift of prayer he gave us the ultimate solution to all of our human problems. Through prayer we find a clue to life's meaning and purpose. We see one another in a new light. Burdens no longer crush us. A new and better world appears on the horizon.

We ask. We receive. Our joy is full.

Chapter 16

MAKING YOUR MARRIAGE
A HAPPY ONE

"What therefore God has joined together,
let no man put asunder."   (*Matt.* 19:6)

A LOVELY scene comes to mind as I write these words.
It was my privilege to readminister their nuptial vows
for a couple who had lived together for fifty years.
Yonder stood these two lovers of many summers and
winters, their eyes bright with a love time could not
dim. Looking at them, I found myself saying, "This is
it. Marriage, despite all the unhappiness associated with
it, can be a success. Life, when shared unselfishly with
another, can be beautiful."

By way of contrast, there was the young couple who
came to their minister to be married, saying, "We have
not thought of buying a home. In fact, we have made
no extensive plans at all. We thought we would see
first how things will work out." *There* you have a

picture of another kind. These two young people, not deliberately insincere, were nevertheless thinking of entering into marriage with the back door open, as though this momentous undertaking were like buying a stove for a trial period.

But don't be too hard on these youngsters; they were only echoing the spirit of an age, fickle, unsure of itself, unstable. There are some words of Shakespeare's which administer the needed corrective to this attitude of casualness:

> Let me not to the marriage of true minds
> Admit impediments. Love is not love
> Which alters when it alteration finds,
> Or bends with the remover to remove:
> Oh, no! it is an ever-fixed mark
> That looks on tempests and is never shaken.

And again,

> Love's not Time's fool . . .

The instability of marriage in our time is revealed in the following figures: from 1900 to 1940, there was an increase of 73 per cent in population (in our nation), 121 per cent in the number of marriages, and 374 per cent in the number of divorces. Dr. Hazen Werner quotes the words of David Cohn, that "divorce lightly

asked and lightly granted is individualism gone mad."[1]
Let those who seek happiness in marriage enter it with
something *more* than a question mark in their minds.

One of the most beautiful stories ever written is in
the twenty-fourth chapter of the book of Genesis. If I
were a film producer I would want to portray this rare
bit of domestic history with reverence and understanding. It is the account of the wooing of Rebecca.

Crafty old Abraham summoned his favorite servant
and dispatched him to Mesopotamia to seek out a wife
for his son Isaac among their kinfolk. This servant, let
us note in passing, was one of the finest "matchmakers"
that ever lived. He possessed a shrewd eye, rare common sense, and consummate tact. In reply to the old
servant's question, as to whether or not she would
accompany him on his return journey, Rebecca made
her forthright and simple reply, "I will come."

As the old servant and the maiden approached, Isaac
went out to meet Rebecca, realizing that it was she who
would share his life with him. How beautiful the sequel,
as stated in the grand simplicity of the King James
Version of the Bible: "And Isaac took Rebecca to his
mother Sarah's tent; and she became his wife and he
loved her."

At the beginning of this chapter, we stated our
conviction that married home life can be happy and

[1] Hazen Werner, Real *Living Takes Time* (New York, Abingdon-
Cokesbury Press), p. 61.

rewarding. That assertion, however, needs to be quali-
fied with certain, indispensable safeguards. Suppose
that now we consider a few of these safeguards—spiritual criteria, let us call them—of happy marriage.

I

Let those who seek happiness bring the attitude of
reverence to the marriage altar. We need to define
again the original purpose of Christian marriage: no
silly slapstick romance but an adventure in mutual
understanding on the part of two people with a Christian home and children in mind.

In its highest reaches, marriage becomes sacramental,
a veritable union of body, mind, and soul for time and
eternity. God help us to get back to that basic and
noble concept, for nothing less than the home life of
our nation is at stake.

A Roman Catholic archbishop has lately ruled that
musical selections of a lighter vein be barred in marriage
ceremonies in churches of his jurisdiction. *O Promise
Me, I Love You Truly,* and *Through the Years* are to
make way for the more sonorous and somber strains of
Palestrina. Perhaps the churchman is on the right track.

However that may be, it would seem that something
more important than the quality of *music* is at stake in
the performance of the marriage rite. This has to do
with the motive of those who approach the marriage

altar. This rightful intent is contained in the chaste and solemn words of the marriage service as found in the *Book of Common Prayer*. What a shame that they should ever be repeated irreverently and accepted lightly.

Let us imagine, for a moment, a bride and groom standing at the altar and giving their consent to these words:

> To join together this man and this woman in holy matrimony, which is an honorable estate, instituted of God, signifying unto us the mystical union that is betwixt Christ and his church.

Later in the same service, there appear these cautioning words:

> And therefore, is not by any to be entered into unadvisedly or lightly; but reverently, discreetly, advisedly, soberly, and in the fear of God.

The institution of marriage—"this holy estate," as the Prayer Book terms it—needs to be entered into with becoming respect and reverence.

I recall a very unhappy couple who came to their minister with a problem. The initial ardor of their marriage had perceptibly cooled. They were at the breaking point. And yet, they could not help but feel the legitimate restraints and the deep soul searching involved in making their final decision. One of them asked, "Doesn't it say somewhere in the marriage ceremony that what God has joined together man must not put asunder?" One could only reply, "Yes, it does. But did you make sure, in the first instance, that God had something to do with bringing you together?" The casual and flippant manner with which marriage is sometimes regarded is not only an affront to God but a menace to society.

Bear in mind again the words at the heart of the Marriage Service: Not "unadvisedly or lightly, but reverently, discreetly, advisedly, soberly, and in the fear of God."

When his friends commended him on the self-sacrificing manner with which he cared for an invalid wife, a man replied: "At our wedding, I took my mate for 'better or for worse, for sickness or for health.' " And he added, "It has not been so difficult after all, for I love my wife."

II

Here now is a second condition of happy marriage, one which people often overlook. A happy, eventful marriage is by no means a happenstance, an accident. It is the result of careful and painstaking nurture. Two people have put their "backs" into it. The marriage relationship, at best, is often a frail and tender plant to begin with, one which needs the caress of sunshine, light and summer rains. And, irony of ironies, there are people who show more solicitude for a dog, cat, or automobile than for a life mate!

The epitaph that might suitably be erected over many a matrimonial casualty is this: *died of neglect.* Said a noted psychologist, as we were talking over the telephone, "I see so many couples who are unhappy who do not need to be."

Sometime ago the *Readers' Digest* ran a series of articles on marriage in which husbands and wives were allowed to air their complaints. Let it be added that they took full advantage of the opportunity. A wife insisted that the American husband gives his wife everything but love. A noted Hungarian psychiatrist was quoted to the effect that American husbands and wives *want* to love each other but do not know *how.* There is doubtless some value in getting complaints about marriage out into the open. And yet, one cannot help feeling that something of a much deeper nature is involved in marital felicity than emotional and physical knowhow.

Perhaps the problem of many younger couples could be stated somewhat like this. Once the honeymoon is over and the humdrum life has begun, Mary makes the discovery that her John is a *mortal* after all and hardly the Prince Charming she thought him in their courting days. His kisses are no longer so ardent. What is more, he carries dirt in on her newly scrubbed floors, scatters cigarette ashes all over the place, and puts his feet on her favorite chair. Lately, he seems to have forgotten to take her places. Worst of all, he has committed the unpardonable sin of forgetting their wedding anniversary.

And, let it be said, John may have a few complaints on his part. He finds Mary's cooking to be quite average, not quite so good as his mother's. And Mary is careless in her spending and not as neat in her housekeeping as he had hoped.

What has happened is that both Mary and John have been omitting the little meaningful "extras" that count for so much in a home. Actually, they are still in the process of becoming acquainted. The poetry of marriage has vanished somewhat and the prose stage has arrived. When it comes to forgetting the little courtesies and extras, as we have called them, let us admit that men are the greater offenders.

In *A Mid-summer Night's Dream* Shakespeare states the plight of many a young bride in the early stages of her disenchantment:

> We cannot fight for love, as men may do;
> We should be woo'd, and were not made to woo.

There was the happy husband and wife I met on one occasion, experienced veterans of the 'holy estate' of matrimony. When I asked for their secret I was told that they begin each day with a resounding quarrel. "But we haven't told you all," replied she. "You see, that leaves us all the rest of the day to make up!"

III

We come now to this third essential to happy wedded life: the need of magnanimity and a forgiving spirit when the need arises—and arise it will.

The fact that the institution of marriage still stands as a monument is due to the many thousands who still believe in and practice this spirit of forgiveness. When couples come to a counselor and ask, "Do you think our marriage has a chance to survive?" The answer might well be, "Yes, providing you are willing to forgive, to live and let live." For it is not so much the size of the problems people confront as the size—the moral stature—of the people themselves that determines the outcome.

In the fine lines of Whittier,

> For still in mutual sufferance lies
> The secret of true living.
> Love scarce is love that never knows
> The sweetness of forgiving.

Making Your Marriage A Happy One

Let Elizabeth Barrett Browning tell us of her love for her poet-husband in some of the most beautiful lines ever written:

> I love thee to the level of every day's
> Most quiet need, by sun and candlelight.
> I love thee freely, as men strive for right;
> I love thee purely, as they turn from praise.

> *　　*　　*

> I love thee with a love I seemed to lose
> With my lost saints. I love thee with the breath,
> Smiles, tears, of all my life!—and, if God chooses
> I shall but love thee better after death.

And let us not label such words "sentimental." Would that there were more of this kind of "sentimentality" abroad in homes today. No mask worn over the face, no grudges held or confidences unshared.

I once read this beautiful tribute the famous singer, Lauritz Melchior, paid his wife Kleinchen, as he affectionately calls her.

> I have lived happily, because I have had a wonderful companion at my side—my wife—and we have learned to square ourselves with each other. We know that in order to have a real partnership in marriage, we must each have our own individuality.

Melchior continues,

> We took up our life structure hand in hand, and my
> darling Kleinchen has been my inspiration, my comrade,
> my love and my guiding angel now for over twenty-
> six years.[2]

In a day where there is so much disillusionment
about marriage, such words deserve to be framed and
hung in plain sight.

IV

This essay on happiness in marriage would not be
complete without an added word. No marriage—and
no home life—can be ultimately secure *unless it is
anchored deep in the love and grace of God*.

Human love by itself is not enough. This is almost
to utter a truism; and yet, how many need to be
reminded of it. Only love that finds its fruition in God
abides. A young bride was overheard to say, "But I
do not feel any need for the church; I feel all my needs
met in my love for my husband." One could only feel
sorry for her. The time will come when she will find
that her house of love has been built on sand.

[2] Lauritz Melchior, *This I Believe op.cit.*, p. 117.

And the rain fell, and the flood came, and the winds blew
and beat against that house, and it fell; and great was
the fall of it.   (*Matt.* 7:27).

Enduring homes and marriages are built on rock,
not sand.

Some of us know whereof we speak. We think not
only of the happiness of our homes but of the parental
homes in which we were reared. There were no expensive paintings on the walls or Brussels carpets on the
floors of these homes. Nor was there a dietitian's chart
displayed at the family table. I have sometimes said
that my mother never bothered to count calories—she
counted noses!

But something there *was*—in that childhood home of
ours—substantial, solid, granitic. There was the mutual
love and devotion of two comrades who had proven
their worth through many a summer and winter, joy
and sorrow. I can remember two such sterling persons,
on a cold winter night, sitting quietly and contentedly,
side by side, in our humble Minnesota parsonage. And
a little lad near by felt a deep inner security as a result
of this fidelity, one which has lasted through the years
and has seen him through many a hard stretch in his
adult life.

One of the most eloquent tributes I have ever heard
was paid by a man to the wife of whom he had recently
been bereaved. "If I had to do it all over again," he said,

"I would want it to be the same, would want her by my side. And do you know, parson, I look forward to spending an eternity with her, in the love of God."

We can have happy Christian homes, providing we are willing to pay the price. The tuition consists of reverence at the marriage altar and mutual love and forgiveness in the years that follow.

This above all: make Christ the center of your home —the Silent Listener to every conversation, the Unseen Guest at every meal—and your happiness will be assured.

Chapter 17

KEEP GRATITUDE ALIVE
IN YOUR HEART

"And one of them, when he saw that he was healed,
turned back, and with a loud voice glorified God."

(*Luke* 15:15).

DWIGHT L. MOODY once told of an elderly man who
gave testimony at one of his meetings. He had lived
most of his life on "grumble street" he said. But after
he became a Christian, he moved to "thanksgiving
street." The joy of his gratitude was written all over
his face.

It would be a good thing for each of us to ask himself this question at least occasionally: have I a thankful
heart? For, if we do not, we are hardly worthy of the
name Christian.

Let me suggest this definition of a Christian. He is
one who responds, with all of his faculties—including
that of thankfulness—to God's gift of life in Jesus Christ.

He lives on "thanksgiving street." He knows the lines of a much-loved hymn:

> Come, Thou Fount of ev'ry blessing,
> Tune my heart to sing Thy grace;
> Streams of mercy never ceasing,
> Call for songs of loudest praise.[1]

The need for thanksgiving is dramatically illustrated in Jesus' encounter with the ten lepers. Dr. Luke, who was evidently an eye witness, tells us what happened on that occasion. The Master was crossing the boundary between Samaria and Galilee on His way to Jerusalem, when He met these lepers. Pathetic creatures that they were, they hailed Him at a distance, lifted their emaciated stumps of hands, crying, "Jesus, Master, have pity on us!" Responding with the compassion so typical of Him, Jesus healed them, suggesting that they repair to the temple and show themselves to the priests.

Then, alas! Nine of the ten lepers hurried from the presence of their benefactor with the thoughtlessness so characteristic of the world, without so much as a word of thankfulness. One of them, however, and he a despised "foreigner," redeemed the situation. No sooner was he aware of his healing than he turned back and exultantly *shouted* out his glory to God. What is more, he thrust himself upon his face at Jesus' feet and,

[1] From the hymn "Come Thou Fount of Every Blessing," by Rev. Asahel Nettleton, 1825, *Inter-Church Hymnal*, p. 123.

mingling tears with his words, poured out his tribute of gratitude.

One out of ten—*there* you have it! What a vignette of thanksgiving! A 10 per cent return on a 100 per cent investment, so another has described the happening. The nine lepers were just *thoughtless*. Therein lay the tragedy.

We are not surprised that the Master should exclaim, "Were not ten cleansed? Where then are the *nine?* Only this stranger has thought to give God glory!" Jesus stands aghast at the ingratitude of nine men who a moment ago had been the very off-scouring of society and whom God in His mercy had healed.

Perhaps this spiritual *imbalance* is the root cause of much that is wrong with us in the world today. Call it what you want—the subject of this chapter—the "anatomy of thanksgiving" or something of the like. But none will deny that the theme is deserving of prayerful consideration.

I

According to Jesus it is not enough for us merely to feel the warm glow of gratitude. Our thanksgiving is not complete *until it is expressed*. It must become vocal. Only then does the river flow back to the sea.

Albert Schweitzer has some extenuating words concerning the nine lepers who went away without thanking Jesus. After all, he says, they must have felt inwardly grateful. They merely failed to express publicly what they felt. The great missionary goes on to say that the gratitude of many of *us* is like that: like water that flows beneath the earth and needs to come to the surface that it might refresh the parched lives of men.

Jesus, however, offers no such alibi for the nine. Ultimately, there can be no excuse for ingratitude. When the warm surge of thanksgiving prompts you to offer praise, you are to obey. Gratitude is a sublime grace when addressed to the one who has blessed you. So insisted the most grateful soul that ever trod our earth.

This subject, we begin to see, opens up horizontally on the lackluster quality of modern life. Something is lacking there—tragically so. Many a discouraged man speaks often of it: the hard, brittle anonymous, competitive—suppose you furnish your own adjective—character of life in modern society.

What is it that is lacking? I will hazard a guess. The average one of us is too vocal with his complaints and too close-lipped and "cagey" when it comes to the simple grace of *appreciation*. We are like the man Charles Lamb said he saw in a dream, standing at the lowest rung of a ladder stretched towards heaven and exclaiming, "I want, I want!" The sin of acquisitiveness gnaws at our vitals. And if, by chance, anyone who reads these words thinks himself an exception, let him be on guard. "Let him that thinketh he standeth, take heed lest he fall."

You see, there is so much more to thanksgiving than merely being "nice" to each other. It goes deep into the heart of our need. For lack of gratitude we are emotionally ill. The ingrate, whatever else may be wrong with him, is a sick individual. The thankful person is the healthful person.

A young minister told me recently of a reticent parishioner who could hardly bring himself to say a kind word about the sermons he heard in his church, from Sunday to Sunday, even though it was evident that he had been helped by them. To give his pastor an occasional "pat on the back" would be going sentimental. He was content—as are so many others—to stifle his feelings and damn a good thing with faint praise.

One is reminded of a certain church deacon who prayed, "Lord, bless our dominie. You keep him humble, and we'll keep him poor."

I am suggesting that we practice the fine art of appreciation and begin *as close in* as the elevator boy and the milk man, to mention but a few of the anonymous host who labor to make life worthwhile for us. For if a man thank *not* his brother whom he has seen, how shall he thank God whom he has not seen? The vertical and horizontal dimensions intersect in vital thanksgiving.

I am one who believes that half of the ills that afflict human beings in our day would disappear were we to retrieve the grace of thanksgiving to God and appreciation toward our fellows.

II

We moderns also blunder in taking our most cherished blessings for granted, forgetting that the "other side" of a great blessing is a great responsibility. We need Goethe's reminder that each generation must win anew its basic freedoms. There is a sense in which we must begin again at scratch.

In this push-button era of ours, we need to pray a twofold prayer. Let the first be distinctly personal: "God, keep me from the sin of personal pride. If life has smiled on me; if I have enjoyed reasonably good health and a modicum of success in my chosen work; if I have been blessed with love in my home circle, let it not go to my head. Keep me humbly grateful." Charles Edward Jefferson used to say that gratitude is born in hearts that take time to count mercies.

The fact is that we are pensioners on a divine bounty. Jesus reminded His disciples that the very hairs of their heads were numbered, that others had labored and they were the beneficiaries. Actually our very lives are lent to us. Why, then, should the spirit of mortal man ever be proud?

One of my favorite stories is about a man who always boasted of being self-made. A disgusted acquaintance of his finally came up with this reply: "If, as you say, you are self-made, you certainly relieve the Lord of a lot of embarrassment!"

The prayer we pray for ourselves we ought also to pray for our nation. Let us sing not only "God bless America," but, what is more, "May America always be deserving of divine blessing." One marked difference between us and the nation's founders is in the spirit of humility.

The beloved comedian, Will Rogers, once said that the Pilgrims were grateful because they were alive, free, and had something to eat. We, in contrast, feel ourselves unfortunate if we do not drive an expensive car, wear the latest style clothes, and live on a government handout. The false give-away motif of many of our radio and television programs is helping to destroy the moral fiber of a people which is being indoctrinated with the vicious idea of *something for nothing*.

Dr. Arnold Toynbee, British historian, warned Americans recently that they need to renew the spiritual *roots* of their heritage. We are in danger, that is, of becoming a cut-flower generation, of going to seed through moral erosion. A nation is on the decline when God, as a living reality, is no longer enshrined at the center of its culture, when it mistakes mere technological advance for progress.

This is to say that we should thank a kind Providence for our moral and spiritual heritage, with its bestowal of life and freedom, and secure it by sharing it with the enslaved of the earth and by transmitting it to our children. That duty is paramount and obligatory on us all.

When he spoke at the Pilgrim Festival in New York in 1850, the great Daniel Webster "put words" in the mouth of Elder Brewster. We need to be reminded of them.

> ... You who are our descendants, who enjoy prosperity and the thousand blessings showered upon you by the God of your fathers: We envy you not. Be prosperous, be enlightened, if such be your allotment on earth; but live, also, always to God and Duty. Accomplish the whole of your great destiny. And if it be that through the whole you still cherish an undying love for civil and religious liberty—and are willing to shed your heart's blood to *transmit* them to posterity, then will you be worthy descendants of Bradford, Standish, of Winslow, and the rest of those who landed from stormy seas on the rock of Plymouth.[2]

[2] Pamphlet, *News Letter*. The Congregational Christian Society, Fall, 1955.

That accent of thanksgiving not only as an expressed grace but as a sacred trust as well, has almost *paled* on the American people. And we had better retrieve it lest our heritage of life go to seed. We need a new race of *Mayflower* descendants who will trace their relationship to their historic forbears by more than blood ties. Let it be repeated: we need to renew the roots of our heritage. That was what Woodrow Wilson meant when he remarked that America needs to be spiritually reborn if she is to endure physically.

Thanksgiving as a sublime entrustment—blessings attended by responsibilities—surely that thought should challenge every grateful person among us.

III

we show how much the grace of God means to us.

Let us dare to go one step further and think of thanksgiving in its deepest dimension: as an *overflow of heart*. That means that the depth of our gratitude will reflect the extent of our experience of God's grace.

The Samaritan leper fairly shouted his praise and glory to God because he experienced this deeper dimension of healing. He knew, as every experiential Christian must know, what had happened to him when he met Jesus. The Master had done so much *more* than heal his body: he had been healed of leprosy of soul, had had instilled in him again the will to live, had become *whole*. And when that miracle of rebirth happens to a man, he cannot but fling himself at the feet of his benefactor, "lost in wonder, love and praise!"

I, for one, find this deeper dimension noticeably absent from much contemporary thanksgiving. It is muffled at its heart and lips. It knows no bounding note of joy, no overflow. It is calculating, cumbrous, and pedestrian, a once-a-year affair rather than a sustained attitude of praise and adoration. There is a story that St. Francis once lodged for a night with a stranger. His host, eager to listen in on the devotions of the famous saint, pressed his ear to the keyhole of the door behind which his guest would pray. One expression of rapture, only, could he make out, and that continued all through the night. The saint kept repeating, "O God, God, God!" Rapture!

Was not *that* what the Samaritan leper felt, once Christ had made him whole? And do *we*—do you think —possess that note of grateful rapture in our religion today? Above all, the inward experience of God's amazing grace which alone can create such praise? Or, are we middle-of-the-road Christians leaving that to the Pentecostals? I wonder!

One thing, however, is certain. If we *do* possess it, this deeper dimension of thanksgiving will sweep everything else into its orbit. It will enable us to lay our very sins, sorrows and burdens at the feet of the Master and leave them there. Like those first Pilgrims at Plymouth, we will weave the very stuff of our sufferings into our garland of praise to the Most High. Like Sarah Adams, after her kindling experience of Heaven's love, we shall be able to say,

> So by my woes to be,
> Nearer my God to Thee.

Years ago in Maine there lived an invalid minister who conducted a weekly radio program which brought help and cheer to many listeners. Few of his hearers, however, knew of this man's personal predicament, that he had been bedridden for fourteen years, that he was blind.

In a letter to a friend, he wrote, "Thank God, my anchor holds. I can no longer move, but I can pray and praise." People said that just to stand by his bed and feel the impact of his radiant spirit was better than listening to the most eloquent sermon.

Keep gratitude alive in your heart. Try living on "thanksgiving street." Reckon up your mercies and you will feel an inner kindling of soul. People will be glad at the sight of you. And who knows? Perhaps even the heart of the infinite Giver of every good and perfect gift will rejoice.

Chapter 18

WHAT ARE YOU EXPECTING?

"My soul, wait thou only upon God; for my
expectation is from him."   (*Psalm* 62:5).

IF LIVING is to be enduringly exciting, we need to keep
the spirit of creative expectancy alive within ourselves.

I recall visiting a home which fairly bustled with
this spirit. A new life was soon to make its earthly debut
there. Parents and children had entered into a con-
spiracy of mutual love and service. We call it
"expecting."

Actually, we are all expecting something from life.
And we *usually get what we expect*. There is an unwritten law inscribed by an unseen Hand: life rewards
or penalizes us in accordance with the nature of our
expectations. As the marriage ceremony has it, "For
better for worse, for richer for poorer." So it is with
our expectations.

What Are You Expecting?

There are two statements in the Bible which are unique in the range of their meaning and appeal. We unconsciously pattern our lives on the basis of one or the other. The first is from the book of Job: "The thing which I greatly feared is come upon me." (Job 3:25). Here we see life attuned to fear. The second is in Psalm 62: "My soul, wait thou only upon God; for my expectation is from him." (Ps. 62:5). These words, by way of contrast, point the way to faith, confidence, poise and power.

Did we only realize it, we are dealing with "dynamite" in discussing this quality of creative expectancy. There is no power quite like it. It is one of those spiritual imponderables that makes the difference in men. Get it into your life and you will accomplish the hitherto impossible. Hidden possibilites will spring to light.

Says the Psalmist elsewhere, "I was as a wonder to many." (Ps. 71:7). Or, as we colloquially put it, "He's a wonder." Creative expectancy, which in the last analysis is just faith at work in a life, is the handle with which we take hold of life.

Now ponder again these two statements from the Bible and then ask yourself on the basis of which philosophy you are building your life. The two texts actually "preach" their own sermon. All we have to do is to inject illustrations of their truth from the book of everyday living.

I

We see the pivotal importance of creative expect-ancy, first of all, when it comes to faith in God. We live by fear or by faith, and our lives get made up accordingly.

For instances of the fear and doubt attitudes we need only to look about us. The most tragic waste of all is to be found not in industry but in human lives—lives that were meant, like some swelling chord, to march on to a climax of achievement but which were tripped up by doubt, fear, cynicism.

Dr. Elton Trueblood is right in saying that the para-mount need of our day is for fellowships of moral sensitivity, faith, and joy, which abhor escapism and demonstrate the power available at the heart of the Christian gospel. The Christian faith, he says, is accepted intellectually and formally, but somehow has failed to fire the imagination of people. Faith might well be described as the golden key which unlocks the treasure house of God.

Three centuries ago Thomas Goodwin made the statement that Jesus is the greatest believer that ever lived. He turned the quality of faith loose in the lives He touched. By means of its magic alchemy he made nobodies into somebodies, transformed defeats into victories. When, at the foot of the Mount of Transfiguration, the father of the epileptic said to him, "If you can—help us," the Master replied, "What do you mean, 'If you can?' Everything is possible to a man if he will believe." There were no "ifs" in the religion of the Son of Man.

I find in my ministry that if I can get people to *let* His power come into their lives through vital expectant faith, there is no limit to what they can become. The same primitive gospel which so spiritually revolution-ized that ancient Mediterranean world re-enacts itself again in actual lives and situations.

When the disciples saw the mighty signs and miracles Jesus performed they were filled with wonder, and exclaimed, "Lord, increase our faith!" Notice that they did *not* ask for their burdens to be lightened. They asked for vital and victorious faith. He is the wise Christian, who, when he prays, does not ask for things, success, popularity, worldly possessions, but for the gift of life-giving faith. For that gift includes all other gifts. What we need to do is to get our expectations *right*. Ask yourself again and again: "What am I expecting?"

II

This spiritual law that we get what we expect in our quest for life operates with amazing dependability when it comes to the *ills of the body and mind*. "The ills that I greatly feared have come upon me." Lowell once said that the important thing is the kind of world we carry around inside ourselves, that everything else takes its hue and color from that.

Illustrations of this basic truth abound. A hospital patient told me, with noticeable pride, that she suffered from an "Eisenhower heart." I could only say to her, "I hope that you have an 'Eisenhower faith and courage' to overcome your difficulty. This woman had identified her ailment, whether real or imaginary, with that of a dynamic personality, thereby giving it an importance it would not otherwise possess.

A friend of mine has an elderly aunt who visits in his home every fall. During the first part of every November, she expects—and gets—a severe cold. Nature can be most obliging and seldom disappoints her suppliants.

I have always been grateful that I was reared in a home in which children were taught to love, rather than to fear, nature. Nature with her processional of seasons, her myriad moods and her rich bounty was not an enemy to us but a friend.

My father, like Theodore Roosevelt, was an ardent advocate of the strenuous life. He would have scoffed and hooted at the false solicitude with which well-meaning but unwise parents surround their children in this day.

What Are You Expecting?

In one of his poems, Edwin Markham vividly describes what went into the making of young Abe Lincoln.

> The color of the ground was in him, the red earth,
> The tang and odor of the primal things—
> The rectitude and patience of the rocks;
> The gladness of the wind that shakes the corn;
> The courage of the bird that dares the sea;
> The justice of the rain that loves all leaves;
> The pity of the snow that hides all scars;
> The loving kindness of the wayside well.[1]

Nature knew her man and out of her bounty toughened him for the hard tasks that lay ahead.

A minister friend tells of entering the hospital room of a man who had lost the will to live. Doctors and nurses had done their best but had almost given him up. Maybe, they suggested, a spiritual practitioner could offer a ray of hope. My friend stood prayerfully by the bedside of this man and quietly but firmly repeated some of the great promises of the Bible: "The Lord is my shepherd, I shall not want." "My soul, wait thou only upon God; for my expectation is from him," and others. He then prayed a prayer of simple but believing faith, leaving the patient completely in God's hands.

A few days later the sick man was sitting up and before long was on the sure road to recovery and

[1] Edwin Markham, "Lincoln, the Man of the People," *Quotable Poems, op. cit.,* p. 216.

health. What is more, he knew from what source his healing had come. Christian faith had made its immemorial appeal to deep, God-given resources lying dormant in the subconscious mind of the patient and had stirred them, like so many red corpuscles, into action. Deep had called unto deep. A full healing resulted.

I believe that we have barely *touched* the hem of the Great Physician's garment when it comes to ministering to the ills of the human mind and body. The greatest and most revolutionary discoveries lie ahead.

III

This law of creative expectancy functions, too, in our *human relationships*. I can walk among my fellowmen with my fist clenched and ready to strike or with hand extended to bless.

A discerning friend has a theory according to which we all send out vibrations of love or hatred, good will or animosity. And what we send out comes back to us. Expect pettiness, meanness, selfishness from your neighbor and you help to create it. Fortunately, the opposite is also true.

> Give, love, and love to your heart will flow,
> A strength in your utmost need;
> Have faith, and a score of hearts will show
> Their faith in your word and deed.[2]

[2] Madeline Bridge, "There Are Loyal Hearts."

What Are You Expecting?

Here again it is the world within ourselves that plays the decisive role, that becomes the arbiter in our inter-relationships. Like appeals to like, deep calls to deep.

In our home we once had a little dog who was amazingly sensitive and responsive to human moods. She would bark furiously at one man who used to walk by our house shouting threats and throwing sticks. She would respond with affectionate eagerness to still another man who was fond of animals and spoke kindly to her. Those of us who are pet lovers know that animals react in kind to love or hatred, kindness or brutality. They seem to feel our "vibrations."

Speaking of human relationships, it has been said that President Eisenhower's presence at Geneva accomplished more lasting good for international relationships than the combined efforts of our most clever statesmen. There is about the Eisenhower personality a downright warmth and friendliness that appeal to people. In the long run, genuine Christian character and personal sincerity are our finest national assets. Human beings, whether white or black, red or yellow, respond *in kind*.

A hospital nurse gave as her opinion that a genuine smile and a friendly handshake have more curative value than long and tedious prayers in the sickroom.

IV

Finally, this spirit of creative expectancy is indispensable in our work for God and His kingdom.

In his poem *The Right Must Win*, Frederic William Faber begins by saying,

> O, it is hard to work for God,
> To rise and take his part
> Upon this battlefield of earth,
> And not sometimes lose heart.

A little farther on he describes the decisive importance of faith:

> Thrice blest is he to whom is given
> The instinct that can tell
> That God is on the field when he
> Is most invisible.[3]

If we do not believe that God is "on the field," we go about our Christian tasks with empty hands. We are beaten at the start.

A young minister once complained to Phillips Brooks of a lack of progress and concrete results in his work. "Are you expecting conversions when you preach?"

[3] Frederic William Faber, "The Right Must Win," *Favorite Poems*, Elmo ed. (Chicago, Belford, Clarke & Co., 1888), p. 233.

asked the great preacher. The younger man confessed that he had not been. "You must expect them," came the reply of experience, "and then you will have them."

Christian workers in our day need to pursue their tasks in the spirit of a Charles Haddon Spurgeon, who said: "The gospel enables us to venture great things." No amount of human talent or ecclesiastical acumen can ever take the place of the God-appointed means for success. Said the Apostle Paul: "But we have this treasure in earthen vessels, to show that the transcendent power belongs to *God* and not to us. (II Cor. 4:7).

We are in need of the faith of a William Carey, father of the modern missionary movement. While still a boy William Carey asked religious leaders of his day what was being done to take the gospel to the heathen. He was told to sit down and be quiet. The indomitable young believer never surrendered his vision of taking the Good News of Jesus Christ to those who had never heard it. He cobbled shoes for a living. People referred to him as the "shoemaker preacher." The time came when Carey was invited to address a company of British clergy on his favorite subject. It was on that occasion that he uttered words which became the slogan of Christian World Missions in their infancy: "Expect great things from God, attempt great things for God."[4]

Shame on our petty little efforts for God! We should

[4] Quoted by Julia H. Johnston, *Missionary Heroes* (New York, Revell, 1913), p. 45.

dare *great* plans for God and the Kingdom and then carry them through to completion, relying on the Strength that never fails. "Expect!" "Attempt!" Here we have the twin heartbeats of great spiritual achievement.

When we worship in the church of our fathers, let us dare to turn our faith loose. Dare to believe that Christ waits to accomplish a truly great work in us and through us. Let us *honor God with great expectations*.

To sum up, believe in God with a vibrant living faith. Let the healing forces of the universe come to you and bring their healing to mind and body. Walk among your fellowmen with love and goodwill in your heart. In your work for God keep expectancy and faith at the helm.

Say often to yourself, "My soul, wait thou only upon God; for my expectation is from him."

Chapter 19

WHY FEAR DEATH?

"... And deliver all those who through fear
of death were subject to lifelong bondage."

(*Hebrews* 2:15)

MY FRIEND, Jeoffrey O'Hara, the distinguished composer and song writer, likes to tell how he came to write his great hymn, *There Is No Death*.

The song stems from a conversation which he had with a colonel who had served at the front during the First World War. This officer had lost most of the men of his regiment during an exceedingly bloody encounter. He told of the extreme desolation and stench of death on every side as he walked along the trenches.

Then a remarkable thing happened. A message seemed to come inwardly to him, as if from on high: Your men are not dead. They live. They flank you on every side. They live and breathe and love. This man turned to O'Hara and said. "I tell you, Sir, there is no death."

If only we all possessed that sublime note of assurance! But many in our day seem to lack it. In the second chapter of the New Testament Epistle to the Hebrews, the writer speaks of those who all their lifetime are subject to bondage through the fear of death. Think of dragging life out like that—in perpetual fear and dread of the day of your demise.

Louis the XV of France never allowed the word "death" to be spoken in his hearing. Nor did the late William Randolph Hearst. The subject was taboo.

In our age of aspirin and barbiturates, that which should be regarded as triumphant translation has been surrounded with the accent of the morbid. Our escapist generation does not like to face up to the facts, in particular the fact of death.

While I was being engaged for a funeral service recently, a relative of the deceased said, "We want to get it over with as soon as possible." That is, by no means, an uncommon request in our time. We even want our funerals snapped up!

The late Joshua Loth Liebman told of a family in his parish who sought to soften the experience of death in the home for their children. No word of explanation was given for what had occurred. The children, instead of being allowed to attend the funeral, were whisked away. When they had been returned to their home they were not allowed to ask questions regarding the one who was no longer in their midst.

What irreparable damage we do to the impressionable minds of children when we falsely seek to cushion them from the normal experiences of life!

We need, therefore, to lay a firm hold on the mighty Christian hope as it is contained in this Epistle to the Hebrews. The assurance here is a tremendous one—one into which we may need to *live* our way through personal faith and experience. Jesus Christ, we are told, voluntarily took upon Himself the frailties and sufferings of our human lot, including death, in order that He might deliver all those who are in slavery to abject fear. If we might state a profound truth quite simply, *Our Master, once and for all, plucked fear and defeat from death.* So much so, in fact, that with the Apostle Paul and others of the great Christian saints, we too might be able to say,

O death, where is thy victory?
O death, where is thy sting?

(*I Cor.* 15:55)

Someone has referred to these words as being a "cry from the ramparts of the unconquerable." They are read at most of our memorial services. We need only open our hearts to their sublime meaning. If the revolutionary truth they embody were really to dawn on us, we too could say with our Christian forbears, "Thanks be to God who gives us the victory through our Lord Jesus Christ!" (I Cor. 15:58). And we would never be afraid again.

Let us consider three simple but profound facts in this matter of overcoming the fear of death.

I

Here is the first. What we humans call "death" is actually a normal and natural part of the life process. It is a door that swings open upon eternal life. That realistic book, the Bible, tells us that while we are in life we already partake of the nature of death. You see, that is what the army officer said to Jeoffrey O'Hara: "I tell you, Sir, there is no death. They live."

We human beings, I sometimes think, can learn much from the equanimity and dignity of nature. In her regal calm and beauty she makes no fuss nor flurry. She changes her garments noiselessly. The seasons come and go. And if it be winter now, spring is not far behind.

An Englishman, in describing his impressions of a New England autumn, told of driving through that part of our country and of seeing the lustrous leaves as they shone like pearls on the trees. He ventured the thought that something had to die to bring all that beauty to birth. At the time of frost some basic essence of the tree itself underwent a change—we speak of it as death—in order to provide the splendor of a New England autumn.

Not only from the world of nature can we humans learn but from what we call the "new physics" in our day. Men like Eddington, Sir James Jeans, and others of our deepest thinkers have spoken of the indestructibility of life. Nothing, they are saying, can actually be destroyed, including what we call "matter." It only disintegrates to live again in another form. The great heart of the universe is alive.

Let us go on now from life as we observe it on the inanimate plane to the royalty and dignity of our own beings. You who read these words are the very image and likeness of your heavenly Father. You are not commonplace. Said Tennyson, at the time of his grieving at the death of his friend, Arthur Hallam,

> He [man] thinks he was not made to die,
> Thou madest him and Thou art just.

Add, to the word of the poet, this profound observation out of our great Hebrew-Christian heritage: "He hath set eternity in their hearts."

Living Can Be Exciting

I never cease to thrill at the profound and searching meaning of the Wisdom of Solomon:

For God created man to be immortal, and made him in the image of his own eternity—the souls of the righteous are in the hand of God, and there can no evil touch them. In the sight of the unwise, they seem to die, and their going from us is thought to be destruction; but they are in peace, and their hope is full of immortality: for God hath proved them and found them worthy of himself.

(Wisdom of Solomon 2, 3).

A great hush and an indefinable calm come over any grieving assembly whenever these words are read. Man, the creature of God, *is* an immortal. He is destined for an eternal career.

A boy in trouble once wrote me a letter in which he repeatedly said, "There is something fine and worthwhile deep down inside of me. My task is to bring it to light." Time proved him correct in that assertion about himself.

In our highest hours we all know the sublime truth about ourselves. There is a splendor concealed within us that, like some sleeping princess, needs only to be kissed into life.

I repeat, what we call death is but part of the total life process. We are made for the life eternal. God has set eternity in our hearts.

II

The second fact is that of spiritual progression. I have already made some reference to it. We "die" on a lower plane that we might live on a higher.

This process of constant change takes place on a *physical* level. Biologists say that we get a new body once every seven years. Some of us have already had a whole procession of "bodies." And we need to bear in mind the truth that we are *not* bodies *with* a soul, but souls, living spiritual entities, housed for a few years in a physical body.

I like to think, for instance, of my radiant Christian mother now in her eighties. She has had a whole procession of "earthly temples." And yet there is about her an unmistakable spiritual identity that abides and defies all outward changes of her life—like an old house that has been besieged by many a storm and tempest and yet remains warm and hospitable at its central hearth.

Ben Franklin, one of the most versatile geniuses of modern times, once composed the following epitaph:

Living Can Be Exciting

Like the cover of an old book,
Its contents torn out,
And stripped of its lettering and gilding,
The body of Ben Franklin
Lies here food for worms;
But the work shall not be lost,
For it will (as he believes) appear once more
In a new and more elegant edition,
Revised and corrected by the Author.

The challenge, then, that life brings to us is to keep the inner fires of the spirit glowing and alive. It is—as the poet Holmes insisted—to keep building "more stately mansions" as the "swift seasons" roll their relentless way. There is a gentle hint for us in a line from a letter Dr. Henry Russell Bowie received from a small boy: "I hope you live *all* of your life!" For there is an element of the "unexplored remainder" in all our lives.

Find the Christian man and he is fearless in the face of death. Through God's grace he has already "died" the whole gamut of lesser deaths, above all, to selfishness. The New Testament witness fairly sings out this fact of spiritual progression. "We have passed out of death into life because we love the brethren." (I John 3:14). And again, "For ye are dead and your life is hid with Christ in God." (Col. 3:3). Dr. Emil Brunner refers to this new quality of life as "the cancellation of space-time existence," as time shot through with eternity.

Why Fear Death?

Some worldly wise people seeing an elderly man with radiant face come out of a church on Easter day thought they would have some fun at his expense. "How do you know that your Christ is alive?" they prodded him. His reply was unassailable. "How do I know? I was talking with him just this morning." As someone has said, faith, in the final analysis, has fewer questions to answer than unbelief.

III

Now here is final fact, and in this lies the summation of all I have attempted to say.

In Jesus Christ, the Son of God, death has been abolished, once and for all, and life and immortality brought to light. (II. Timothy 1:10). And, what is more, we become assured of this fact, so confidently and joyously asserted in Apostolic faith, when the living presence of the Risen One has entered into us as sublime reality. The Christian Endeavorers are to the point when they sing,

> You ask me how I know he lives?
> He lives within my heart.

That remarkable Christian statesman, Bishop Hans Lilje, president of the Lutheran World Federation, wrote his book *The Valley of the Shadow* while in a Nazi concentration camp. In this book, an amazing testimony of faith under fire, he says, "To be brought face to face with death gives a certain nobility to a human being." Once fully venture your life, that is, for a cause dear to you, and cowardice and fear are banished. Hear Bishop Lilje again: "So I was able to go through these nightly scenes of hell, which increased more toward the end of the time, without any loss of confidence."

There you have it! Strike out into the darkness of the valley of your shadow, whatever it may be, with faith at your side, and the light shines through. Fear gives way before trust. And out yonder, going toward the Galilees of tomorrow, is the great Captain of our salvation in whose glorious victory we are privileged to share. But the assurance *is to be found only in the venture*.

A friend of mine, a Christian nurse of long experience, told me of the time when she was caring for a patient ninety-two years of age. This patient had a morbid fear of death. Suppose I give you the story in her own words.

"I tried to help her overcome this difficulty. But when I would leave her for the night she would frequently call me back for some reassurance that would bring her through until morning. Each morning she would tell me of her fear and dread of the long night hours. I suggested to her, one day, that she use the words of Bryant's *Thanatopsis*:

> So live that when thy summons comes to join
> The innumerable caravan, that moves
> To that mysterious realm, where each shall take
> His chamber in the silent halls of death.
> Thou go not, like the quarry-slave at night
> Scourged to his dungeon, but sustained and soothed
> By an unfaltering trust, approach thy grave,
> Like one who wraps the drapery of his couch
> About him, and lies down to pleasant dreams.

"However, beautiful as the words were, there was yet an eerie and vague something about them that left my patient uncomforted.

"I also suggested to her that she think of death as a pleasant voyage to a distant and beautiful country to see a beloved friend. Think of the joyous preparation that precedes such a trip. But, again, all my attempts to help her seemed in vain. The fear of death still persisted.

"One evening as I left her, I said, 'Try repeating this line from an old hymn: "*And nightly pitch my moving tent a day's march nearer home.*" [1] '

"The next morning I was greeted with a smile instead of complaints. My patient looked up at me with confidence and told me how much the line from the hymn had meant to her. She said, 'I repeated the words and I

[1] From *At Home in Heaven*, by James Montgomery.

had no trouble because I somehow felt God's arms around me.' Four more years of happiness followed, until finally she pitched her tent in the Father's house."

No, we need not fear death. Let us think of it as a door swinging outwards upon life, infinite and eternal. Live and venture your life, all of it, for a cause that will outlast it. Above all, walk day by day in the company of Him who said, "I am the resurrection and the life."

And then one day you, too, shall say—perhaps with just a bit of impatience—"To think that I ever feared death!"

252.058
M48

Date Due

JAN 27 '58			
JUN 27 '61			
NOV 15 '61			
Nov, 28 JAN 18 '62			
DEC 19 '62			
MAR 28 '63			
SEP 27 '63			
8 '65			
12-16-65			

Demco 293-5   LINCOLN BIBLE INSTITUTE